A Tale of Two Collectors

A Tale of Two Collectors:

The Lithic Collections of
Geoffrey Taylor and David Heys
(with particular reference to
the county of Yorkshire)

Keith Boughey

with contributions by
Alison Sheridan and Fraser Hunter

ARCHAEOPRESS ARCHAEOLOGY

ARCHAEOPRESS PUBLISHING LTD
Summertown Pavilion
18-24 Middle Way
Summertown
Oxford OX2 7LG
www.archaeopress.com

ISBN 978-1-80327-642-7
ISBN 978-1-80327-643-4 (e-Pdf)

This book is available direct from Archaeopress or from our website www.archaeopress.com

"He does not die that can bequeath
Some influence to the land he knows"
Hilaire Belloc (1870-1953) Duncton Hill, Stanza 1

"The archaeologist is not digging up things, he is digging up people"
Mortimer Wheeler (1890-1976) Archaeology from the Earth (1954)

Dedicated to the memory of
Geoffrey Vivian Taylor (1924-1997)

Acknowledgements

I am indebted to many people for their help without which the current work would have been impossible. First and foremost must be Alan Taylor, older son of the late Geoffrey Taylor, who kindly provided me with as much of his father's collection as he could and, since he accompanied his father on many of his trips, was able to provide a considerable amount of useful information, often in the form of his own personal recollections. Secondly, huge thanks to David Heys for allowing me full access to his entire collection and for his memories of his days spent up on the moors with Geoffrey Taylor. Next, I am thankful to Mags Waughman (former Head of Historic Environment, North York Moors National Park Authority), who provided valuable information on Taylor's work with the late Roger Jacobi excavating the Early Mesolithic sites of 'Pointed Stone' and Money Howe; for her many helpful comments and corrections on earlier drafts of this paper; and along with Robin Daniels (Archaeology Officer, Tees Archaeology) for arranging for the entire Taylor Collection to be safely housed at the Tees Archaeology HQ at Sir William Gray House in Hartlepool. Thanks must go to Kim Devereux-West, Dawn Haida and Diane Prest who, on behalf of the North York Moors National Park Authority, carried out the extensive boxing and labelling of material prior to its being sent to Hartlepool. Thanks too to Miles Johnson (Head of Historic Environment, North York Moors National Park Authority) for acting as a much-needed 'conduit' for communications, in particular of earlier drafts of the book.

Moving on to more specialised help, I am hugely grateful to Alison Sheridan (former Principal Archaeological Research Curator of Early Prehistory) and her colleagues at National Museums Scotland, for their help with the jet and jet-like objects in the collections: to Alison Sheridan herself for orchestrating their identification, assessment, photography and illustration, for writing virtually the entire section on jet, and for invaluable comments and corrections of errors elsewhere in earlier drafts of the text; to Marion O'Neil, for her fine illustrations; to Fraser Hunter (Principal Curator of Prehistoric and Roman Archaeology) for information on Iron Age glass bangles; and to Lore Troalen for undertaking X-Ray Fluorescence Analysis (XRF). Thanks too to John and Bob Richardson for checking the identifications of the 400+ lithics, particularly the Mesolithic material, illustrated and discussed in the book. Special thanks also go to Rebecca Tucker (Curator of the W. Hamond Museum of Whitby Jet in Whitby) for being kind enough to examine and evaluate the Late Victorian jet and jet-like pieces, for granting permission to use the map showing the award of jet mining contracts across the North York Moors during the19th century; to the late Helen Muller who first drew the map up, and to Martyn Wright at the Museum, for tracking down its origins; to Elizabeth Blanning, Hon. Curator, Kent Archaeological Society, for information on the whereabouts of the jet bracer (wristguard) from Cliffe; to Torben Ballin, for information on Arran pitchstone and permission to reproduce the map of its UK dispersal; to Rosie Banens, working on behalf of Tees Archaeology, for tracking down and photographing a number of items in the Taylor collection after their transfer to Hartlepool; to Claire Cockrill of the Council for British Archaeology for permission to reproduce the figures illustrating the distribution of battle axeheads across the UK and the North York Moors; and to Terry Manby and John Gilks for additional information on Yorkshire battle axeheads. I am also grateful to Richard Watts (Senior Historic Environment Officer (Records), Lincolnshire County Council) for permission to reproduce and multi-annotate the maps covering sites worked on by Taylor in the Salmonby area of Lincolnshire, as outlined in Appendix 6. Thanks are also due to the following staff at the Archaeology Date Service (ADS) at the University of York for their work in making the Heys collection accessible on-line: Katie Green (who oversaw the entire project), Ray Moore (who oversaw all the digital work), and Catie Teoderescu (University of York student) and Olivia Foster (digital archivist). The work was made possible thanks to a grant from the Open Archaeology Access Fund (OAAF) and the generosity of John Cruse (Secretary) and the rest of the Committee of the Prehistory Research Section of the Yorkshire Archaeological and Historical Society, who generously provided financial assistance with the ADS archiving and with the cost of the jet item illustrations. Any errors which remain, of fact or of interpretation, are entirely my own.

Finally, a special and personal thank you needs to go to my patient and long-suffering wife, Susan, who put up with the obsessive hours I spent on cataloguing, research and writing and my all too frequent frustration, as well as vast numbers of boxes scattered about the house, not to mention the dust!

In addition, I must not forget to give special thanks above all to Mike Schurer, Ben Heaney and Danko Josić at Archaeopress, who did an excellent job getting this book through to publication.

Contents

List of Figures

Chapter 1: The Geoffrey Taylor and David Heys Collections

Chapter 2: Databases and Identification

Chapter 3: Featured Artefacts and Artefact Groups

Chapter 4: Excavations

Picture credits:

The author would like to thank the following for permission to reproduce the following figures. While every effort has been made to trace and acknowledge all copyright holders, we would like to apologise should there have been any errors or omissions. All figures are due to the author, except for the following:

A. Taylor: 1.1, 1.9–1.21, 4.1, 4.12, 4.19–4.20
York Archaeological Trust (P. White): 1.3
Crown Copyright Ordnance Survey. All rights reserved: 1.6, 1.12–1.17, 4.17–4.18, 4.21
T.G. Manby: 4.3, 4.5
Council for British Archaeology: 4.8–4.9
R. Banens: 3.2, 3.13, 3.21–3.23
York Museum Trust: 3.6–3.9, 3.26–3.28
J.A. Sheridan: 3.10, 3.24–3.25, 3.30, 3.32–3.33, 3.35–3.38, 3.40, 3.44–3.55, 3.57, 3.59–3.61, 3.63
T. Ballin: 3.11
Portable Antiquities Scheme: 3.17, 3.19
R. Tucker: 3.29
M. O'Neil: 3.32–3.33, 3.35, 3.38, 3.40, 3.44–3.46, 3.51, 3.58
A. Woodward: 3.39, 3.43
Society of Antiquaries of Scotland: 3.41
National Museums Scotland: 3.42
R. Watts (Lincolnshire Heritage Explorer, Lincolnshire County Council): Appendix 6, 2–5

List of Tables

Preface

The present book does not am to depict or to describe the collections of Taylor and Heys in full, even as far as the county of Yorkshire is concerned. To cover the entire collections and in appropriate detail would take a work of several volumes. Nor does it aim to establish the complete impact of their contents, collected over a lifetime, on UK prehistory, as this would require further programmes of research which could now well be undertaken, involving the use of 'modern' yet what are by now standard techniques of the analysis of material such as X-ray fluorescence (XRF) analysis, radiocarbon dating of charcoal or bone, and the osteological and isotopic examination of human remains such as bones and teeth. What the present book does set out to do, however, is to introduce the collections to the archaeological world and give the reader a clear impression of their contents.

The book begins with brief biographies of the two collectors, outlines the main areas in which they collected, principally the North York Moors, and their method of working, before attempting to set their work into its wider prehistoric context. It then explains how the over 18,000 worked pieces in the combined collections are each individually identified, and presents illustrations of selected groups of pieces, such as arrowheads, knives, axeheads, scrapers and so on. This is followed up with a more detailed look at some of the more notable classes of artefacts, such as discoidal knives, Iron Age glass bangles, and jet pieces including a superb undamaged Early Bronze Age wristguard (bracer), of which only one other example is known in Britain. But to correct the impression that Taylor and Heys only ever collected finds off the surface of the moors and farmland, details of several excavations, most of them never before published, are given. These include pioneering work on the Early Mesolithic of the North York Moors, and the discovery of an Early Bronze Age grave complete with cremated human remains, a decorated Collared Urn and a perforated battle axehead. At long last, the hitherto unheralded work of these two remarkable individuals has been given the long overdue credit it undoubtedly deserves.

K. Boughey
Baildon
December 2022

The Author

A former member of the Prehistoric Society and the Royal Archaeological Institute, the author is an active member of the Prehistoric Research Section of the Yorkshire Archaeological and Historical Society and Hon. Editor of their annual journal *Prehistoric Yorkshire.* His research passion is the prehistory of northern England, particularly the Bronze Age, and especially its rock art. He was a founder member of the Ilkley Archaeology Group and one of the chief contributors to *The Carved Rocks on Rombalds Moor: Gazetteer of the Prehistoric Rock Carvings on Rombalds Moor, West Yorkshire* (1986) and co-author, along with the late Edward Vickerman, of *Prehistoric Rock Art of the West Riding: Cup-and-Ring-Marked Rocks of the Valleys of the Aire, Wharfe, Washburn and Nidd* (2003). From 2008–13, he was Director of the Stanbury Hill Project, an HLF-funded community archaeology project that investigated an Early Bronze Age landscape on Bingley Moor, West Yorkshire, culminating in two publications: *Stanbury Hill Project: Archaeological Investigation of a Rock Art Site* (2013) and *Discovering Prehistoric Bingley: The Stanbury Hill Project* (2013). He has also been instrumental in locating, cataloguing, securing and publishing information on several private collections of prehistoric material, including the complete Lamplough-Lidster excavation archive of around forty Early Bronze Age barrows, excavated in advance of forestation on the North York Moors in the years after World War 2. His more recent publications include (as Editor) *Going Underground: An anthropological and taphonomic study of human skeletal remains from caves and rock shelters in Yorkshire* (2015) and *Life and Death in Prehistoric Craven: Welbury Wilkinson Holgate and the Excavation of the Hare Hill Ring Cairn* (2016).

Chapter 1:
The Geoffrey Taylor and David Heys Collections

Introduction

The world of archaeology naturally depends to a large extent on the work of professional archaeologists, working on behalf of institutions such as Universities or commercial organisations, with ready access to funds and publication. But there is another equally valuable and sometimes under-rated side to archaeology and this is the work done largely by amateurs. Nowhere is this truer than in the field of prehistory, where the efforts of local individuals, often outside the mainstream and working entirely for themselves, can make a significant contribution. This is particularly the case with private lithic collectors, people from many different walks of life who develop a passion, indeed almost an obsession, for collecting flints – work which all too often goes unrecognised and unpublished. At its worst it can amount to little more than looting, removing material without making any proper record of context or provenance and in effect destroying the archaeological evidence it represents but at its best, well provenanced and systematically recorded, it can add substantially and even make a difference to what we know. It is a story of two distinct but interweaving narratives running parallel to each other: on the one hand the story of the collectors themselves and their lives, and on the other the story of what they find and what it adds to our knowledge of the prehistory of any given area.

This book deals with an especially fine example of the better sort of flint collecting – and one that encompassed more than just flints. The modesty of the individuals concerned and their amateur status meant that their work has gone largely unheralded, apart from the accidental discovery and publication of a hitherto unsuspected Early Bronze Age grave assemblage from Low Paradise Farm, North Yorkshire in 1998 (Heys and Taylor 1998), brief mentions by others regarding Taylor's earlier work in Lincolnshire (see Appendix 7), and the odd discursive reference in work published by others (e.g. Jacobi 1978; Manby *et al.* 2003). Friends Geoffrey Taylor and David Heys together and separately over a period spanning almost forty years amassed a combined lithics collection numbering almost 19,000 individual worked pieces covering a huge span of UK prehistory from the Early Mesolithic to the Early Iron Age, mostly from the western, southern and central regions of the North York Moors, but also from the Yorkshire Dales, the Central Pennines (including the Peak District) and Lincolnshire, though the present volume concentrates on the more accessible Yorkshire material, which forms by far the bulk of the two collections put together – over 95% of the material seen. However, for the sake of balance and completeness, an outline of Taylor's earlier work in Lincolnshire is included in an Appendix to the present volume (Appendix 7). Finds covered virtually the complete range of prehistoric tools, from arrowheads, axeheads, blades, burins, knives, microliths and scrapers in flint and chert to pottery sherds, coins and fragments of jewellery in jet, horn and glass.

The book does not am to depict or to describe the collections of Taylor and Heys in full, even for Yorkshire. That would take a work of several volumes. Nor does it aim to establish the full and definitive impact of the contents of the collections, gathered over a lifetime, on the world of UK prehistory, as this would require further programmes of research, involving the use of modern – yet what are by now standard – analytical techniques such as X-Ray Fluorescence (XRF) analysis, radiocarbon dating of charcoal or bone, and the osteological and isotopic examination of human remains such as bones and teeth. What the present book sets out to do, however, is to introduce the collections to the archaeological world and give the reader a good impression of their contents and an indication of their importance for a deeper understanding of the prehistory of at least one part of northern England.

It begins with brief biographies of the two collectors and details of how each of their archives of material can be accessed, outlines the principal areas in which they collected, chiefly the North York Moors, and their method of working, before attempting to set their work into its wider prehistoric context. It then explains how the many thousands of pieces in the collections were each individually identified and presents sample illustrations of selected groups of pieces, such as arrowheads, knives, axeheads, scrapers and so on. But to correct the impression that Taylor and Heys only ever collected finds off the surface of the moors and farmland, details of several excavations, most of them never before published, are given, including the discovery of an Early Bronze Age grave complete with cremated human remains, a decorated Collared Urn and a fine perforated battle-axehead. This is followed up with a more detailed look at some of the more notable classes of artefacts, such as discoidal knives, Iron Age glass bangles, and jet pieces including a superb undamaged Chalcolithic/Early Bronze Age wristguard (bracer) of jet of which only one other example is known from Britain.

Geoffrey Taylor

Figure 1.1: Geoffrey Vivian Taylor 1924–1997

Geoffrey Vivian Taylor ('GVT') (Figure 1.1) was born in 1924 and raised in Bradford. Trained as a wireless telegrapher, he served in the Royal Navy during World War 2 as a Petty Officer on HMS Weston, tasked with escorting merchant ships up and down the west coast of Africa, during which he survived a torpedo attack from a German submarine and a bout of yellow fever! After the war he lived on the family farm, Warlowe Farm (also known as Wallow Camp), near Salmonby in Lincolnshire, where he first cut his archaeological teeth, excavating extensively at prehistoric and Anglo-Saxon sites on this and neighbouring farms, as well as searching for flints in the area. Early on he was encouraged to continue his flinting by Sidney Jackson, then Curator of the Cartwright Hall Museum in Bradford and by F.T. Bahn and F.H. Thompson at the Greyfriars Museum in Lincoln. Eventually he returned to his home town of Bradford, where until retirement he worked for International Harvesters, manufacturers of agricultural equipment, at their Bradford factory in Idle, formerly the site of the Jowett Motor Works.

Conveniently, he was able to make use of stout lidded boxes provided to the company by the firm of Sykes, who supplied gear components, which turned out to be excellent for storing his lithic and other finds. As well as collecting alone, he was often accompanied by his eldest son, Alan, and by Ronnie Pollard, a fellow workmate from International Harvesters. Although a quiet, modest man, Taylor nevertheless corresponded with many of the leading archaeologists of the day, including Stuart Piggott, Ian Longworth, Herman Ramm and in particular Roger Jacobi, with whom he co-operated closely on the excavation of the Early Mesolithic sites of 'Pointed Stone' and Money Howe on Bilsdale East Moor (Jacobi 1978). He died in 1997 (Phillips 1997; Manby 1998a; Alan Taylor pers. comm.).

David Heys

Figure 1.2: David Heys b. 1937

The younger of two children, David Heys (Figure 1.2) was born in Lees, Oldham in 1937. On leaving school, he worked for NORWEB (North-West Electricity Board) as an apprentice before joining Yorkshire Electric as an engineer where he stayed for 31 years until 1991. He then worked for the home-shopping company Betterwear, first as an Area Manager and later in deliveries. His interest in the past was caught when he read Wrigley's local 1911 publication, *Saddleworth: Its Prehistoric Remains*. He first met Geoffrey Taylor in the 1960s while out flinting on the Late Mesolithic site of March Hill in the Colne Valley, which was the beginning of a lifelong friendship. Together for almost every weekend in the 1980s and 1990s, whatever the weather and including New Year's Days, the two men combed farmland directly above Sutton Bank on the western edge of the North York Moors, and either side of the main Helmsley road, hunting for flints, work which was to result in a truly remarkable collection of archaeological material. David Heys now lives in quiet retirement in Springhead, Oldham, curiously part of the former historic West Riding of Yorkshire.

Archive Access

The Yorkshire components of the Taylor collection with which this publication is concerned, numbering almost 17,000 worked pieces and getting on for some 500,000 pieces of waste, is currently stored at Sir William Gray House, the headquarters of Tees Archaeology in Hartlepool, courtesy of their Archaeology Officer, Robin Daniels, pending (at the time of writing) its eventual curation with an appropriate museum. The *digital* archive of the Taylor collection, consisting of an introduction, annotated maps, sites guide, drawings, photographs, diaries and a database giving the details of every piece (including the waste), is currently with the author, pending plans to put it up on-line. The Heys collection, numbering just under 2500 worked pieces, currently resides David Heys at his home in Oldham, as requested. Plans are in place with the collector and his family for this too to be eventually transferred to an appropriate museum. The *digital* archive of the Heys collection, consisting of an introduction, overview, sites guide, database and a complete set of photographs is lodged with the Archaeology Data Service (ADS) at https://archaeologydataservice.ac.uk/archives/view/ lithics_heys_2020 or https://doi.org/10.5284/1062863.

Collecting Areas

The North York Moors, a designated National Park, and one of the chief physiographic regions of Yorkshire, covering over 1400 square kilometres, are formed from a large plateau of Jurassic sandstone rising to a height of some 400m OD dissected by several deep valleys running broadly north-south (Gaunt and Buckland 2003). The total area represented by the collections within the North York Moors conveniently falls into two quite distinct regions (Figure 1.5). The first of these, across the southern and western edges of the plateau and the more sheltered lower slopes, is a predominantly largely flat or gently sloping agricultural landscape. During the time in which the lithics were collected and still today, the area consists mainly of fields for growing potatoes and sugar beet and cereal crops such as winter wheat and barley. Regular ploughing made the flint collecting that much easier and more successful without the need for excavation. Here the bulk of the material collected was from the Late Neolithic through to the Early Bronze Age period. The second of these, the higher central part, is by contrast marked by successive valleys and ridges and mostly (around 40%) typical heather moorland, as well as rough pasture and patches of managed forest. Here the bulk of the material collected was from the Mesolithic.

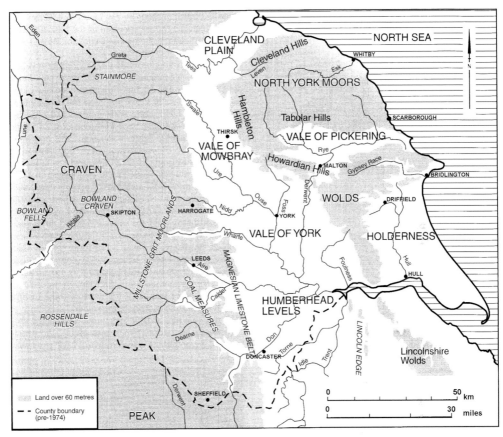

© York Archaeological Trust (drawn by Paula White)

Figure 1.3: Location of North York Moors, showing principal topographical regions across north-eastern England (after Manby et al. 2003, 3 figure 2)

Arguably one of the most distinctive features of the moors, if not of the entire north of England, is their remarkably abrupt western cliff-like edge at 280m OD known as the Hambleton Hills, which drop down through a 30% gradient to the Vale of Mowbray some 200m below at Sutton Bank, giving not without justification what has been described by some authors (e.g. James Herriot) as 'one of the finest views not only in Yorkshire, but in England' (*Ordnance Survey Leisure Guide* 1992, 67) (Figure 1.4). With its high vantage location, commanding views both across the vale below to the west and across the broad gently rising massif of the moors to the E, relatively fertile well-drained soil, light woodland cover with access to water and game, it is perhaps not surprising that the area proved attractive to prehistoric people, who have left plentiful evidence of their presence across this landscape. Useful and comprehensive summaries of the evidence for the period across the whole of the North York Moors and the immediately surrounding lowlands, but which lies outside the scope of this book, have already been provided by Elgee, Spratt, Manby, King and Vyner (Elgee 1930; Spratt 1993; Manby *et al.*

2003: 82–91) and for the Mesolithic period in particular by Waughman (Waughman 2015; 2017) and briefly by Manby (Manby 2013).

Figure 1.4: View of the Vale of Mowbray and Gormire Lake from Sutton Bank (looking west)

By far the bulk (90% 17,507 worked pieces) of the material under consideration comes from 224 sites covering two distinctly different regions of the North York Moors: to the south and west, and across the centre (Figure 1.3, Table 1.1). Further details of each site, too lengthy to be included here, will be found in Appendix 3. They cover the fields occupying the western margin above Sutton Bank on the Hambleton Hills (Sites 1–73) (Figure 1.5: 1, Figure 1.12) and the southern margin overlooking the Vale of Pickering either side of the modern A170 Thirsk-Helmsley road (Sites 74–126) (Figure 1.5: 2–4, Figs. 1.13–1.15) and further east (Sites 142–160) (Figure 1.17) together with a cluster of farms in the Vale of Pickering around Ampleforth (Sites 127–41) (Figure 1.5: 5, Figure 1.16); the rest are on the higher moorland ridges to the north and across the centre (Sites 142–224). It should be pointed out that, although much of the North York Moors National Park is now Open Access land, many of the sites in the Park, particularly those in this region, running south along Sutton Bank and east to Helmsley, lie on private farmland. However, Taylor, as a former farmer himself, was able to visit these sites more or less freely through his personal contacts with the local farmers.

Though Taylor and Heys collected extensively together, they also collected separately on the North York Moors and elsewhere, notably in Heys' case the Central Pennines around his home in Oldham, the Peak District and the Yorkshire Dales and in Taylor's case, from both the Central Pennines, the Peak District and around Salmonby near Horncastle during his time spent in Lincolnshire. These other components of the two collections are worthy of a publication to themselves: indeed, one account of the prehistory of Lincolnshire currently being worked on makes extensive use of Taylor's material gathered during his time there (Chowne forthcoming). However, this book will concern itself principally with the material from the North York Moors.

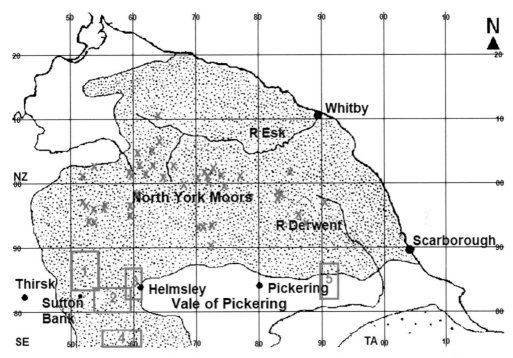

Figure 1.5: North York Moors: South and West Region - Areas of principal interest 1-5 (red rectangles), Central Region - principal sites (either identified or estimated) indicated by X

South and West North York Moors – Prehistoric Setting

However, before launching into a detailed description of the Taylor and Heys collections, it is important first to set their work into its wider archaeological context. The western edge of the North York Moors, where most of their material was collected, is particularly rich in sites and monuments of the prehistoric period (Figure 1.6), especially the Early Bronze Age, and although it is not the purpose of this book to describe this anything like in full it is still worth going into some degree of detail to establish just how important and active an area it was at the time. It is against this sort of background that the collections of Taylor and Heys must be assessed.

The sites along the western edge consisting of assorted round barrows, lithic and pottery finds, and ancient boundaries, but especially the round barrows, mostly now low mounds or completely ploughed out, appear to fall into several loose but distinct clusters (Figure 1.6). The bulk of the sites in the northernmost and central clusters lie in fields belonging to Dialstone Farm. Collectively there is no doubt that they form an Early Bronze Age 'cemetery' taking full advantage of the remarkable location (Denny 1859). As Historic England themselves state: "together the monuments in this area provide important evidence of territorial organisation and the development of settled agricultural practices" (Pastscape). For convenience, they are described in order of these apparent clusters, running from north-south and west-east. For further details of the sites readers are directed to consult the various references given and for the latest information to consult the Historic Environment records (HER) of the North York Moors at http://www.northyorks.gov.uk. Furthermore, many of the sites to be described, beginning in Taylor's time, but continuing into the 1990s especially, now enjoy the protection of Scheduled Monument status (http://historicengland.org.uk/listing-the-list).

No fewer than six round barrows lie in the first northernmost 'cluster': at SE 5064 8832 (Figure 1.6: A) (Pastscape: Mon. No. 57167; Scheduled Mon. No. 1015576), SE 5075 8810 (Figure 1.6: B), SE 5102 8821 (Figure 1.6: C) (Pastscape: Mon. No. 57096), the 'Silver Hill barrow' at SE 5114 8778 (Figure 1.6: D) (Pastscape: Mon. No. 57078, Scheduled Mon. No. 1015575), SE 5151 8821 (Figure 1.6: F) (Pastscape: Mon. No. 57102, Scheduled Mon. No. 1016052), and SE 5194 8821

Table 1.1: Regional distribution of worked[1] pieces

Region	Heys	Taylor[2]	Total
North York Moors S and W	1,118	4,065	5,183
North York Moors Central	649	11,675	12,324
Yorkshire Dales	378	557	935
Central Pennines	86	419	505
Peak District	190	298	488
Lincolnshire	46	–[3]	46
Other[4]	32	27	59
Total	2,499	17,041	19,540

[1]: Dependent on what is meant by the term 'worked': in this case, excluding obvious waste (flakes, fragments, etc.) unless it shows signs of working or re-purposing (e.g. as with blades particularly) though it has to be accepted that whether or not a piece is significantly 'worked' can sometimes be a matter of opinion, so, although the *precise* figures can be disputed, the overall distribution remains clear enough. Individual pieces of waste have not been counted, but one estimate puts the number at 250,000–500,000 (Waughman 2015, 11–12).

[2]: This includes a polished jet ring, originally found by R. Pollard but, since his death, reincorporated into the Taylor collection.

[3]: Not seen or assessed, this component of the Taylor collection – consisting of a large quantity of Beaker, Iron Age and Early Roman sherds – has largely already been returned to Lincolnshire (to Lincoln Museum), and therefore discounted for the purposes of this book (as have similar items in the Heys collection), though it is by no means insignificant to the prehistory of this neighbouring county (see Appendix 7)

[4]: Includes three superb Lower Palaeolithic Acheulian hand-axes – one in the Taylor collection from a gravel pit at Wanstead, East London, found in 1899, and in the Heys collection two from the cliff edge at Barton-on-Sea, Hampshire – as well as several typical Group VI Neolithic axehead roughouts from the Langdale Pike 'axe factory' in Cumbria, a range of cores, blades and scrapers from Hengistbury Head, Dorset, and from several unidentified UK locations, as well as a handful of 'exotic' pieces such as two Maori polished axeheads from New Zealand and a black obsidian knife from Easter Island in the South Pacific.

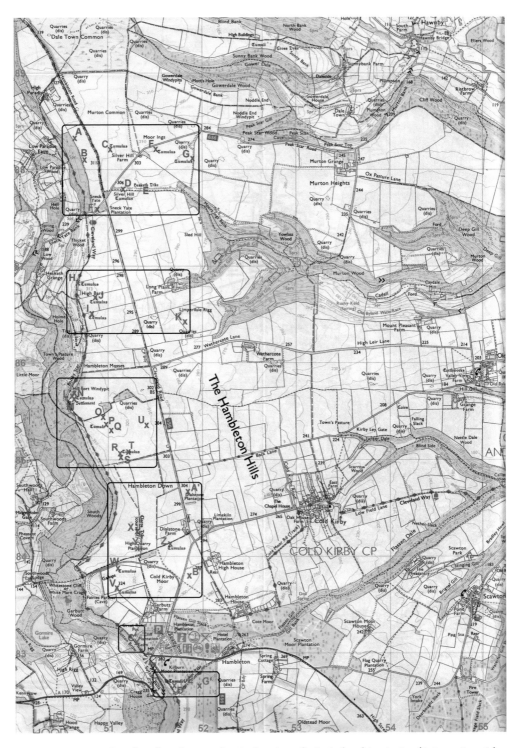

Figure 1.6: Western edge of North York Moors showing locations of principal prehistoric sites (© Crown Copyright Ordnance Survey. All rights reserved)

(Figure 1.6: G) (Pastscape: Mon. No. 57186, Scheduled Mon. No. 1016066). The barrow just above Low Paradise Wood (Figure 1.6: B) was discovered and excavated in 1998 by Taylor and Heys themselves and is described in more detail below (see Chapter 4). Finds included an almost complete Collared Urn containing the cremated remains of an adult male, pieces of flint, charcoal and a superb battle-axehead. Hesketh Dyke centred at SE 5139 8778 (Figure 1.6: E) (Pastscape: Mon. No. 57117, Scheduled Mon. No. 1015575), as with Casten Dyke to the south (Figure 1.6: E′), is part of the Cleave Dyke system, and a well-preserved prominent earthwork, clearly visible from the Boltby-Hawnby road. Stretching some 700m from SE 5103 8789 to SE 5174 8779 it incorporates the 'Silver Hill barrow', clearly respecting its earlier position, running both sides of the barrow but not through it (Spratt 1982: 38) (Figure 1.7).

Figure 1.7: 'Silver Hills tumulus', from W (line of Hesketh Dyke to right)

Next is a group of three round barrows again lying close to the edge of the plateau commanding views over the Vale of Mowbray to the west: at SE 5068 8682 (Figure 1.6: H) (Pastscape: Mon. No. 26901, Scheduled Monument No. 1010535), SE 5082 8650 (Figure 1.6: I) (Pastscape: Mon. No. 57139) and SE 5086 8668 (Figure 1.6: J) (Pastscape: Mon. No. 57136, Scheduled Mon, No. 1009794). Excavated by Denny in 1864, the first of these (Figure 1.6: H) contained a total of seven burials: one, the extended but headless skeleton of what was taken to be a young woman, constituted the central primary burial. A single deposit of cremated remains was found towards the eastern edge. Fragments of three long-necked Beakers (two of which were complete and are now in the Leeds Museum) were recovered from each of the primary graves. Two are thought to belong to Clarke's 'Developed Southern Beakers, eastern cylinder necked variant' and one to his Primary Series Southern Beakers variant (Clarke 1970: 506 Nos. 1242–44) dating to *c.* 2200–1900 BC; in one grave, according to Elgee, the Beaker was associated with the remains of a necklace described as comprising 'over 100 perforated conical and cylindrical bog-oak [sic] beads' close to the woman's skeleton – clearly a much treasured personal item

(Elgee 1930: 55 figs. 14e–f, 56). Curiously, the second barrow (Figure 1.6: I) according to its scheduled classification (Scheduled Mon. No. 1012746) is no longer regarded as an Early Bronze Age round barrow but as a short stretch of Cleave Dyke, constructed at least several centuries later in the Late Bronze Age. A fourth barrow (Figure 1.6: K) (Pastscape: Mon. No. 57142, Scheduled Mon. No. 1009793) lies a short distance away over on the east side of the Cleveland Way at SE 5182 8642 on Limperdale Rigg.

Moving south to the next 'cluster', the principal site here is undoubtedly Boltby Promontory Fort centred at SE 5061 8566 (Figure 1.6: L) (Pastscape: Mon. No. 5712, Scheduled Mon. No. 1013086). A small but typical univallate Late Bronze Age/Iron Age promontory fort, well-sited on a conspicuous bend in the cliff face and known locally as Boltby Scar 'camp', it was investigated in 1938 by G.F. Willmot, the then curator of the Yorkshire Museum, retrieving sherds of Iron Age pottery from the interior and most notably a pair of gold basket-shaped ornaments from under the central section of the eastern rampart. Now in the British Museum, illustrated on-line (https://www.british museum.org/collection /search?keyword=Boltby) and dated by them to c. 2500–2000 BC, they were originally mistakenly thought to be ear-rings but – as with an almost identical pair more famously found in the grave of the 'Amesbury Archer' (Fitzpatrick 2011; https://www.wessexarch.co.uk) – are almost certainly ornaments for the hair. He also excavated two Bronze Age round barrows on the scar at SE 5063 8563 (Figure 1.6: M) and SE 5063 8568 (Figure 1.6: N) (both described at Pastscape: Mon. No. 5712, Scheduled Monument No. 1013086), which although lying well within the interior of the fort had not been unduly disturbed by its later construction (Smith 1994: 103–4 NYM 80–1). A Secondary Series Collared Urn containing cremated bone and charcoal was recovered from the primary position of the more northerly barrow (Figure 1.6: N) (Longworth 1984: 239 No. 1089). Sherds of two further vessels, most probably Collared Urns, were retrieved from the southern side of the more southerly barrow (Figure 1.6: M) (Smith 1994: fig. 65.3), along with flints, charcoal and a piece of worked jet. One of the barrows was effectively bulldozed to the ground to bring the site into cultivation in 1961 (Elgee 1930: 157 and fig. 54; Challis and Harding 1975; Spratt 1993: 101 table 21, 124–6) while the other remains severely mutilated.

There follows a set of five round barrows, three of which (Figure 1.6: O, R and T) are much reduced by the plough: at SE 5093 8543 (Figure 1.6: O) (Pastscape: Mon. No. 57151, Scheduled Monument No. 1010341), SE 5097 8536 (Figure 1.6: P) (Pastscape: Mon. No. 57151, Scheduled Mon. No. 1010342), SE 5102 8530 (Figure 1.6: Q) (Pastscape: Mon. No. 57151, Scheduled Mon. No. 1013085), SE 5112 8507 (Figure 1.6: R) (Pastscape: Mon. No. 57154, Scheduled Mon. No. 1010343) and SE 5121 8508 (Figure 1.6: T) (Pastscape: Mon. No. 57148). The third of these (Figure 1.6: Q) is most probably the 'Grooms Stool' barrow excavated by Denny in 1865, which yielded two Collared Urns (Spratt 1993: 101 table 21). The fourth of these (Figure 1.6: R) is the so-called 'Lord Barrow', named after its excavator, Thomas Lord. At the centre of the mound was the contracted skeleton of a girl in her early teens, accompanied by an inverted Beaker (Clarke's Primary Southern Group c. 2250–1900 BC) (Smith 1978), two stone 'tools', a used quartzite pebble and 13 pieces of flint including a leaf-shaped point (Smith 1978; 1994: 105–6 fig. 70 NYM 84; Spratt 1993: 82 table 14). Located immediately south of this barrow, with which it may be associated and visible on aerial photographs, is a pit alignment at SE 5113 8502 (Figure 1.6: S) (Pastscape: Mon. No. 1032907, Scheduled Mon. No. 1010345) of probable Late Bronze Age/Iron Age date forming part of the Cleave Dyke system. A Mesolithic shouldered point and, prompted by Heys, an impressive collection of Late Neolithic/Early Bronze Age arrowheads were also recovered from this area, described as 'Hambleton Down' by Meegan (Meegan 2009; 2011). An impressive group of sherds of Neolithic Rudston-style 'Peterborough' (aka 'Impressed') ware (dating most probably *c.* 3300–2900 BC) were found by Lord at 'an unknown plough-damaged location' in one of the fields east of Boltby Scar, possibly at SE 507 859 according to some sources (Spratt 1993: 81 table 12; Manby *et al.* 2003: 50 fig. 18, 51) but most probably the one reported at SE 5140 8535 (Figure 1.6: U) (Pastscape: Mon. No. 57160), where the finds also included a Group VI axehead, reinforcing the Neolithic association, and several pieces of jet (Hayes 1963a). Immediately outside the 'cluster' across the Cleveland Way to the east, on land belonging to Long Plain Farm, a group of flint arrowheads and spears were found between 1904 and 1910 at SE 5168 8538 (Figure 1.6: A') (Pastscape: Mon. No. 57299). Sadly, no further details are available as to their precise identity or current whereabouts.

Built on a false crest, now surmounted by a triangulation pillar, a round barrow formerly known as 'Dialstone cairn' at SE 5108 8368 (Figure 1.6: V) (Pastscape: Mon. No. 25563, Scheduled Mon. No. 1010344) was first excavated by Greenwell before 1859 and again in 1864, though oddly there is no published report of any finds (Denny 1859; Hayes 1963b; Department of the Environment 1978). The next barrow, at SE 5110 8389 (Figure 1.6: W) (Pastscape: Mon. No. 25590, Scheduled Mon. No. 1018550) (Figure 1.8), also set on a false crest, was excavated by Verity in 1863. An urn, half full of cremated remains, and fragments of an Accessory Vessel were found surrounded by clay, charcoal and burnt bone. A short distance to the north lies a further round barrow at SE 5128 8429 (Figure 1.6: X) (Pastscape: Mon. No. 1525708), much reduced in height but still visible on air photographs, on top of which a World War 2 air-raid hut was built, giving the name of 'Hut Field' to the field in which it sat by Taylor, which proved to be one of his most prolific collecting sites. In 1992, Taylor carried out a brief excavation at a site estimated as SE 5130 8408 (Figure 1.6: Y) where he uncovered a scatter of cremated bone, charcoal, pottery, flint and chert, probably associated with one of the burials in the area and disturbed by the plough. The 1856 OS 1:10560 map shows three other 'tumuli' in the area (OS 1856). Tot Lord was said to have dug into three mounds centred on SE 5164 8413 (Figure 1.6: Z) (Pastscape: Mon. No. 57299) according to local farmers and there is allegedly a Beaker from this area in the Lord collection at Settle Museum. Lord also found Iron Age sherds north of Dialstone Plantation at SE 5184 8466 (Figure 1.6: A') (Pastscape: Mon. No. 57367), while to the west of Hambleton House crop-marks visible in air photography centred on SE 5184 8378 (Figure 1.6: B') (Pastscape: Mon. No. 1525698) revealed a set of linear and curvilinear field boundaries covering an area of approximately 10ha believed to be part of a Romano-British settlement.

In the final southernmost cluster, there are two round barrows, both excavated by Greenwell in 1864. From the first at SE 5129 8312 (Figure 1.6: C') (Pastscape: Mon. No. 57333, Scheduled Mon. No. 1012742) just flint chippings and charcoal were found but nothing else (Greenwell 1865: 115; Greenwell and Rolleston 1877: 337–8 Barrow CXXVII; Kinnes and Longworth 1985: 90 No. 127; Spratt 1993: table 21, 101). The second at SE 5169 8267 (Figure 1.6: D') (Greenwell 1865: 115–16; Greenwell and Rolleston 1877: 338–9 Barrow CXXVIII) (Pastscape: Mon. No. 57330, Scheduled Mon. No. 1012744) revealed two burials: a Primary Series Collared Urn containing the cremated remains of an adolescent (Longworth 1984: No. 1106) under the centre of the barrow and a Secondary Series Collared Urn (Longworth 1984: No. 1107) containing the cremated remains of an adult to the east-south-east, along with a small thumb/horseshoe scraper, flint chippings, sherds and charcoal (Kinnes and Longworth 1985: 90 No. 128, plate

Figure 1.8: 'Gallops tumulus' (from the south)

128; Spratt 1993: 101 table 21). The area also contains two clearly visible components of the Cleave Dyke system: Casten Dyke North runs for 0.2km from SE 5165 8256 to SE 5210 8293 (Figure 1.6: E') (Spratt 1982: 42) (Pastscape: Mon. No. 57368, Scheduled Mon. No. 1012992) while one stretch of the Cleave Dyke runs from north to south through almost the entire length of the area from SE 5089 8759 (Figure 1.6: F') to SE 5196 8265 (Figure 1.6: G') (Pastscape: Mon. No. 1032865). The system was constructed between the Late Bronze Age and Iron Age acting as a set of territorial boundaries to augment the natural divisions of the terrain. On Hambleton Moor the course of the dyke appears to have been defined by the pit alignment (Figure 1.6: S) and the two barrows (Figure 1.6: R and T), weaving first to the east, then to the west, to avoid them, pointing at its later construction (Denny 1859; Heys 1963; Moorhouse 1978a; Spratt 1982), before passing just to the east of two further barrows (Figure 1.6: X and Y).

N.B.: Although the site details are unchanged, 'Pastscape' entries have now been superseded by Heritage Gateway entries, both managed by Historic England.

Locations of sites

Dialstone Farm

A word first about one particular area which stands out above the rest. Turning to the first major area of collection – the south and western edges of the North York Moors – this is dominated by material from the fields surrounding Dialstone Farm (Sites 10–29) (centred on SE 5182 8427) (Figure 1.9) just above and to the north of Sutton Bank lying alongside the old drove road formerly known as 'Hambleton Street' (Elgee 1930: 103) and now forming part of the Cleveland Way. These fields proved to be an extraordinarily rich hunting ground for the two collectors, particularly two Taylor named 'Car Park Field', from a small car-park still extant at the eastern edge of the field alongside the Cleveland Way (Sites 22–23) (centred on SE 5120 8530) (Figure 1.10), and 'Hut Field'(centred on SE 5140 8481) (Sites 18–21) (Figure 1.11), named after a now demolished World War 2 air-raid warden's hut built on the top of a ploughed out round barrow at SE 5128 8429.. Car Park Field alone contributed 1768 worked

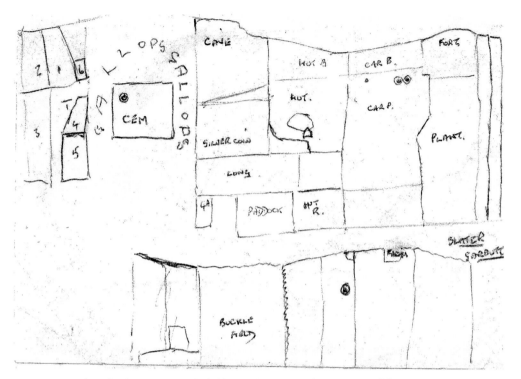

Figure 1.9: Taylor's sketch map naming the fields at Dialstone Farm (Locations 10–29) (south–north left to right, distance approx. 3km)

pieces to the Taylor collection and Hut Field a further 477 pieces, together representing 55% of all the worked pieces from the region. 31% of Heys' total haul for the region (348 out of 1118 pieces) was again from these same two fields.

For example, to concentrate on just one type of material whose use is highly significant in the prehistoric period – jet – the figures speak for themselves, as shown in Table 1.2 below. The figures are broken down into worked pieces (just one of which is possibly not prehistoric but Victorian), indeterminate pieces which may or may not be worked, and natural pieces of unworked jet.

In other words, these two fields alone accounted for over half of all the jet items collected and for almost two-thirds of those that were worked, figures which are unlikely to be due to coincidence or chance. Similar, though less striking, comparisons can be made for other types of artefacts, such as arrowheads or scrapers.

According to a well-known saying in archaeology absence of evidence is not necessarily evidence of absence, but in this case presence of evidence is undeniably evidence of presence. It could be argued that the sheer number of visits they made to just these two sites – 266 out of a total of 744 (36%) recorded visits between December 1983 and June 1997 – resulted in such a large number of finds: on the other hand, putting the argument into reverse, it could be that it was the large amount of material found here that attracted them to make so many visits.

Figure 1.10: View of fields surrounding Dialstone Farm looking north along the Cleveland Way – 'Car Park Field' (Site 23) to the left

Figure 1.11: 'Hut Field Bank' (Site 18) looking east from the south-west corner of 'Hut Field' (Site 20) viewed from Whitestone Cliff Edge (Radio mast indicates centre of Dialstone Farm just over the skyline)

Table 1.2: Distribution of jet pieces

Site	Worked pieces	Indeterminate	Natural	Total
Hut Field	8	4	11	23
Car Park Field	15	3	15	33
Other (i.e. all other sites)	13	12	22	47
Total	36	19	48	103
Hut Field and Car Park Field as % of total	64	37	54	54

However, the fact remains that these two fields, covering a combined area of just over 10ha, alone represent over half of all the material Taylor and Heys collected from the entire region: 2593 out 5183 worked pieces. Both the size and the sheer diversity of the material point to this being an area of special significance throughout the post-glacial prehistoric period, but especially in the Early Bronze Age. In fact, it is reliably reported that many of the local farmers formerly held (or possibly in some cases still do hold) their own private collections of prehistoric flints, especially the more notable pieces such as arrowheads.

Identification of sites

The collections together covers sites in some 354 named sites (Appendix 3), 224 of which cover the North York Moors alone. However, neither of them made any use of map references, preferring instead in the case of the farmland in the southern and western region of the North York Moors to reference finds on according to the field in which they were found. These were named after either the farm or the farmer to which they belonged, followed usually but not always by a particular distinguishing feature of the field. Thus, for example there are references to 'Dialstone Cemetery Field' (Figure 1.9), '40A (i.e. Forty Acre) Field', 'Observatory Field', and so on. Based on these names, along with sketch-maps and other distinguishing features occasionally mentioned by Taylor in his diaries and further features on Ordnance Survey maps (such as tumuli, radio transmission towers and the like), the author was gradually able to identify most of the fields with confidence and the remainder with reasonable certainty. The locations shown on the maps below and listed in Appendix 3 are therefore those of the author.

For finds on the moorland plateau to the north however, details are unfortunately much less precise. While some of these can be pinned down to a specific location, in most cases they do little better than designate the general area. However, a summary of no fewer than sixty-three separate sites where Mesolithic material was found on the higher ridges by Taylor, broken down into 'Early', 'Late' and 'Very Late', has already been provided by Spratt (Spratt 1993: 54–5 table 2, 64–5, table 4, 66 table 5), though it only gives 'approximate' locations to the nearest 100m and is now regarded as somewhat out of date. Taylor's Mesolithic sites on the high moors have now largely been established by the work of the North East Yorkshire Mesolithic Project, led by Waughman (Waughman 2015). Hence, it is the farmland sites, indicated in Figs. 1.12–1.17 below, that inevitably tend to form the main focus of this book.

Maps

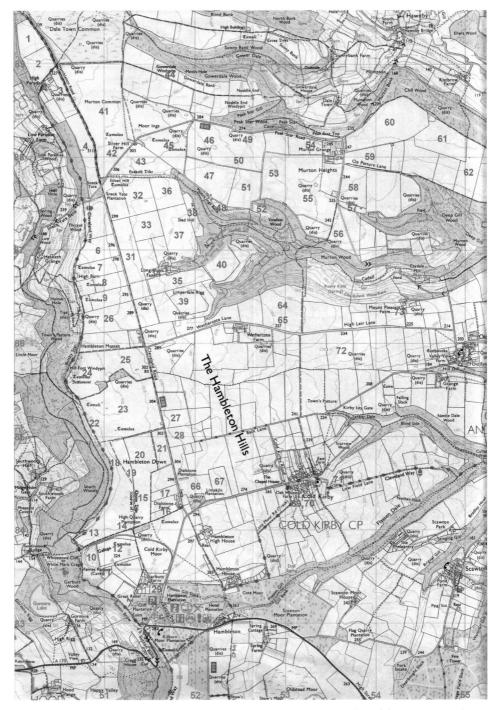

Figure 1.12: Locations 1–73 (Locations 29, 30, 63, 68 and Valley View Farm off-map) (© Crown Copyright Ordnance Survey. All rights reserved)

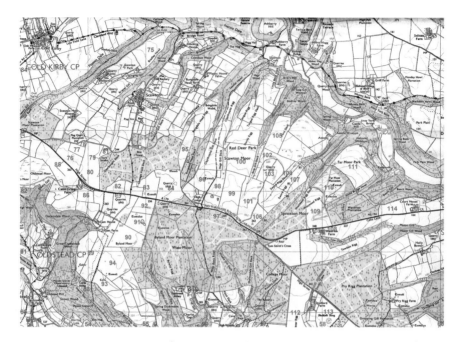

Figure 1.13: Locations 74–114 (© Crown Copyright Ordnance Survey. All rights reserved)

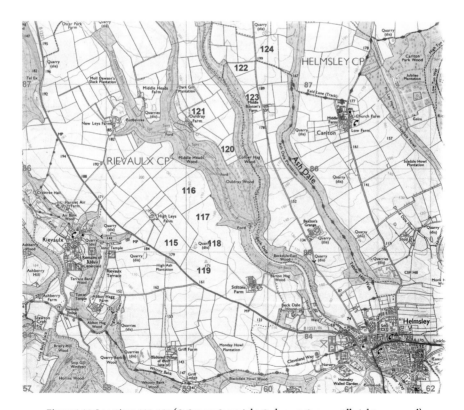

Figure 1.14: Locations 115–124 (© Crown Copyright Ordnance Survey. All rights reserved)

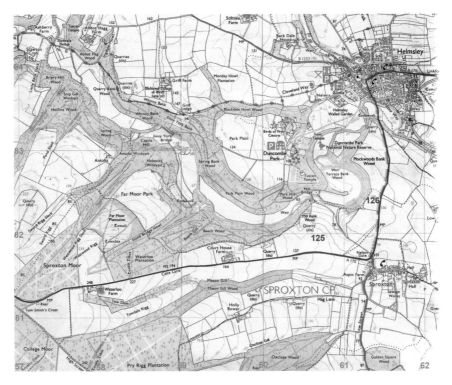

Figure 1.15: Locations 125–126 (© Crown Copyright Ordnance Survey. All rights reserved)

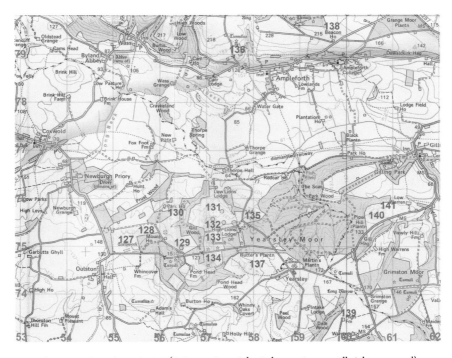

Figure 1.16: Locations 127–141 (© Crown Copyright Ordnance Survey. All rights reserved)

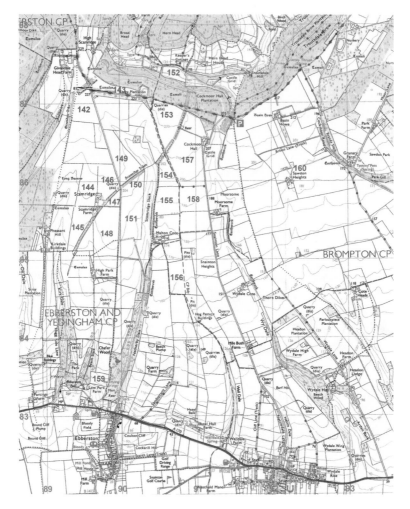

Figure 1.17: Locations 142–160 (©: Crown Copyright Ordnance Survey. All rights reserved)

Recording and Illustration

Over such a lengthy period of collecting and with such frequent visits, Taylor and Heys gradually got to know most of the farmers of the southern and western area and gain their trust, which in turn aided their collecting efficiency and success. Finds were fully described, mapped to their precise location within each field and skilfully illustrated by Taylor in a series of 118 exquisite drawings (e.g. Figs. 1.18–1.19) and in four handwritten diaries covering the period from December 1983 to June 1997, along with anecdotal remarks about the weather and, reflecting his former life as a farmer, the prevailing crops, of which the extracts shown below are typical (Figs. 1.20–1.21). Collectively, the four diaries form an invaluable personal record of their collecting activities during the period. These are especially valuable as Heys himself did not keep any formal written record of his finds, apart from scraps of information written on the matchboxes in which he kept his finds – as, for example, in the case of the fine Neolithic foliate knife fragment and the relevant diary entry below (Figure 1.22).

Entries read:

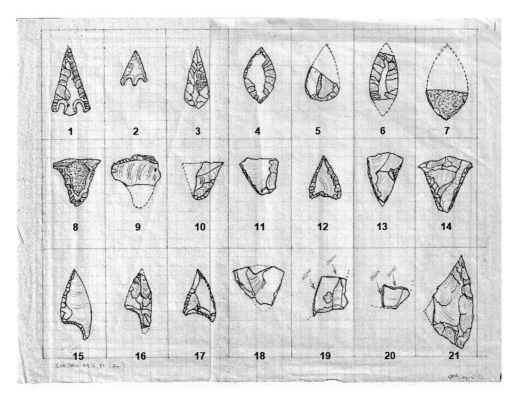

Figure 1.18: Drawings of lithics, Sheet 1 (arrowheads) (23: Car Park Field, Dialstone Farm) (Taylor)

1   T2.2.11.2   *barbed-and-tanged arrowhead*
2   T2.2.12.12   *barbed-and-tanged arrowhead*
3   T2.2.12.6   *leaf-shaped arrowhead*
4   T2.2.12.10   *leaf-shaped arrowhead*
5   T2.2.11.4   *leaf-shaped arrowhead (proximal fragment)*
6   T2.2.12.7   *leaf-shaped arrowhead*
7   T2.2.11.5   *leaf-shaped arrowhead (proximal fragment)*
8   T2.2.12.5   *transverse arrowhead*
9   T2.2.11.8   *unidentified arrowhead (fragment)*
10 T2.2.12.8*   *transverse arrowhead (longitudinal fragment)*
11 T2.2.12.3   *transverse arrowhead*
12 T2.2.12.11   *leaf-shaped arrowhead*
13 T2.2.11.7   *transverse arrowhead*
14 T2.2.11.3   *transverse arrowhead*
15 ?   *British oblique arrowhead*
16 T2.2.12.9   *British oblique arrowhead*
17 T2.2.12.4   *British oblique arrowhead*
18 T2.2.11.6   *transverse arrowhead*
19 T2.2.11.9   *transverse arrowhead (distal fragment)*
20 T2.2.11.10?   *transverse arrowhead*
21 T2.2.4.2   *unidentified arrowhead (fragment)*
: note further drawing of this lithic below (Fig. 1.19: 9)

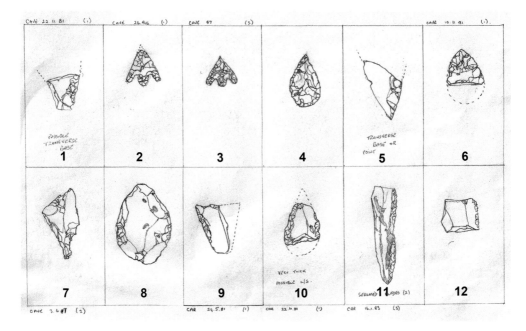

Figure 1.19: Drawings of lithics, Sheet G (Dialstone Farm) (Taylor)

1	T1.16.3	transverse arrowhead (proximal fragment)		13: Cave Field, Dialstone Farm
2	T1.83.1	barbed-and-tanged arrowhead		20: Hut Field, Dialstone Farm
3	T1.114.1	transverse arrowhead		"
4	T1.114.2	leaf-shaped arrowhead		"
5	T1.114.4	transverse arrowhead (proximal fragment)		13: Cave Field, Dialstone Farm
6	T1.114.3	leaf-shaped arrowhead (distal fragment)		"
7	T1.66 1	transverse arrowhead		"
8	T1.66.2	leaf-shaped arrowhead		"
9	T2.2.12.8	transverse arrowhead (longitudinal fragment)		23: Car Park Field, Dialstone Farm
10	T2.2.19.2	leaf-shaped arrowhead (medial fragment)		"
11	T2.1.4.1	plano-convex knife		"
12	T2.1.3.7	serrated knife (fragment)		"

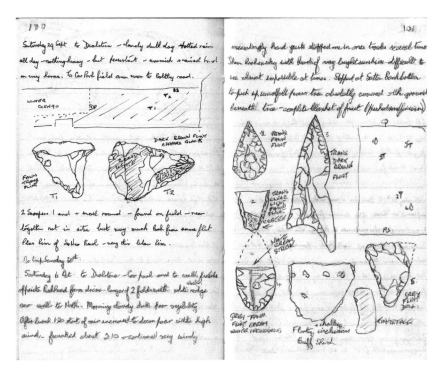

Figure 1.20: Diary 2, pp. 100–101 showing entries for 29th September and 6th October 1990 (note sketch maps indicating the locations and detailed drawings of each find)

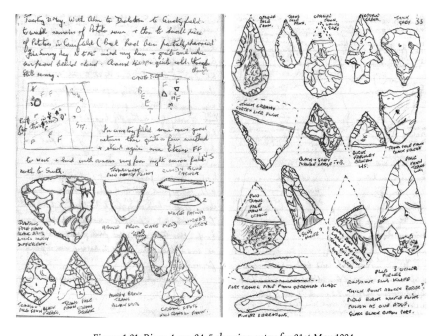

Figure 1.21: Diary 4, pp. 34–5 showing entry for 31st May 1994

Diary 2:

"Saturday 29 Sept. To Dialstone – cloudy, dull day, spotted with rain all day – nothing heavy – but persistent –warmish and rained hard on the way home. To Car Park field area over to Boltby road. 2 scrapers (1 end and 1 small round) found on field – near together, not *in situ* but very much look as if they are from the same flint, plus rim of Sec. Neo. Bowl – very thin below rim. Map & Drawings.

Saturday 6 Oct. To Dialstone – Car Park and to walk fields opposite Redhead's farm drive – about 2.10 p.m. and continued very windy, increasingly hard gusts stopped one in one's tracks several times, then broken sky with bursts of very bright sunshine – difficult to see, almost impossible at times. Stopped at Sutton Bank bottom to pick up windfall pears – tree absolutely covered – the ground beneath the tree a complete blanket of fruit (picked some for wine). Map & Drawings."

Diary 4:

"Tuesday 31 May. With Alan to Dialstone to Cemetery field to walk remains of potato rows and then to small piece of potatoes in Cave field (Beet had been partly sharried). Fine sunny day N to NE wind very keen and quite cool when Sun passed behind cloud. Around 4.00.p.m. quite cold though still raining. In Cemetery field some rows good returns then quite a few without and start again area between Fort field to west and band with arrows right across field north to south."

Figure 1.22: Foliate knife/dagger (Heys collection: H787.1) (Site 83#)*
(: for explanation of lithic numbers, see below Chapter 2: Identification of individual lithics)*
(#: for full details of sites, see Appendix 3)

Entry from Taylor Diary for 5th January 1988 (Diary 1, p. 125) reads:

> "White Barrow field – sown corn – little flint on surface. Newly ploughed field at road-side – freshly done – not had time to erode yet but some flints found. Crossed road to small field – scrapers found here. *David found piece of a large knife [Figure 1.22]*. G.V.T. half an arrow-type? Ripples suggest probable transverse. Drawings." (author's italics).

Chapter 2:
Databases and Identification

Databases

The entire Heys collection, the smaller of the two, containing only worked pieces, but covering all of the sites both inside and outside the North York Moors, has been entered into a single database. However, the Taylor collection, much the larger, containing both worked pieces and waste, progressively came to light in batches over a considerable period of time, including a fine set of purposely built display trays. Each of these batches was originally perforce catalogued separately and the items entered into separate databases, giving rise to no fewer than twenty-two databases, each covering a different region or combination of regions. However, these were all combined later into a single master database covering all the discovered material Both database, covering unique number, description, date and location of each find, along with links to photographs (Appendix 4) and to entries and illustrations in Taylor's own diaries (Appendix 5), are much too large to be included here, but are given in full in Appendix 1. However, examples of typical database entries for both collections are given below:

Heys Database:

Box	No.	Date	Diary	Location	Figure	Photo	Description
115	2	1995.02.19	4.65–6	23: Dialstone (Car Park Field)	4.65. D2	Set 3	barbed-and-tanged arrowhead

Taylor Database:

Database	Tray	Box / Bag	No.	Date	Diary	Location	Figure	Photo	Description
1	-	75	3	89.03.04	2.7	20: Dialstone (Hut Field)	2.7√	T1.75.3	jet ring or pendant
2	7	17	1	before 92.04.25	3.59	93–4: S of Cold Cam Farm	-	Tray 7 T2.17.7.1 (1 –5)	polished Gp. VI axehead

Identification of individual lithics

Each individual item is uniquely identified by reference to its place in the collection and the database as explained below:

Heys Collection

H for Heys
1st no.: No. of box within which the lithics are stored
2nd no.: No. of item in each box
e.g. (as per entry above)
H115.2: Heys Database, box 115, item 2 is a barbed-and-tanged arrowhead

Taylor Collection

T for Taylor
1st no.: No. of original database
2nd no.: No. of tray (if applicable) within which the lithics are stored
3rd no.: No. of box/bag within which the lithics are stored
4th no.: No. of item in each box/bag
e.g. (as per entries above)
T1.75.3: Taylor Database 1, box 75, item 3 is a jet ring or pendant
T2.7.17.1: Taylor Database 2, tray 7, box 17, item 1 is a polished Gp VI axehead

Analysis of the Taylor and Heys Collections

Having dealt at length with the scope and geographical range of the Taylor and Heys collections, it is time to analyse the material in more detail and to describe some of the more remarkable and noteworthy pieces. There are several ways of approaching any such analysis but the way adopted here is to combine both type of item and site in a single analysis, as follows. This has been done by collating the information from all the databases into a single set of tables, each table dealing with a different set of sites (available in the archive). Of course this is only really possible if the locations are known with sufficient precision and certainty, as with the vast majority of the material collected in the south and west region. Unfortunately, except for a few specific sites where Taylor excavated or was assisted in the excavation of specifically named and identified sites such as 'Pointed Stone' and Money Howe (both with Jacobi), this has not really been possible for most of the remaining central region of the moors to the north, where for the most part only the general area of the location is indicated. These will therefore be dealt with separately.

However, a few words of caution are needed before approaching any such analysis. The collection includes vast amounts of waste, particularly for the Mesolithic material, numbering (according to one estimate) well over 500,000 pieces! Firstly, what was collected depended on the methodology of the two collectors, which in Taylor's case was virtually total, including worked pieces and fragments as well as waste, while Heys tended to concentrate on only complete worked pieces, particularly arrowheads. Their technique was generally surface collection with occasional trowelling beneath the surface, apart from a handful of occasions when a proper and systematic excavation of an entire site was carried out (e.g. Boltby Urn site, 'Pointed Stone' and Money Howe). To a very real extent, therefore, the number of lithics collected in any one location could simply reflect its popularity or ease of access and be directly related merely to the number of visits. Secondly, it depends on precisely what categories of artefact are defined and how, and being able to identify accordingly what any particular piece is – not always obvious, especially when only fragments remain. In what follows, only the broadest of classification has been used, based on both complete and near complete pieces as well as fragments, to give an outline picture of distribution and period. More detailed subdivision along typological lines, e.g. into the various classifications of arrowheads by Green (Green 1980), or of microliths or scrapers, has not been attempted. That awaits further research and a further publication. However, the more remarkable and archaeologically significant items will be picked out, not only to illustrate the wealth and diversity of the two collections (e.g. a remarkable Chalcolithic/Early Bronze Age 'wristguard' of jet) (Taylor 2.7.12.1), but to add what is considered to be important information to the archaeological record.

What follows in this and the following chapter are photographs of selected pieces (Figs. 2.1–2.16) – a mere fraction of each collection – chosen both to highlight the individual pieces themselves as well as to illustrate the excellence and diversity of the two collections. They are accompanied by their unique numbers (as explained above), their location and where appropriate in the following chapter with information and discussion as to their wider archaeological context (e.g. Late Neolithic discoidal knives, Early Bronze Age battle-axeheads, Iron Age/Romano-British glass bangles etc.). In the current chapter, however, their purpose is therefore essentially illustrative. Where three or more different types of arrowhead are present, they are in some cases simply described as 'assorted' arrowheads; similarly, the term 'borer' has been used in a generic sense to describe tools which might well be borers, gravers, points or burins.

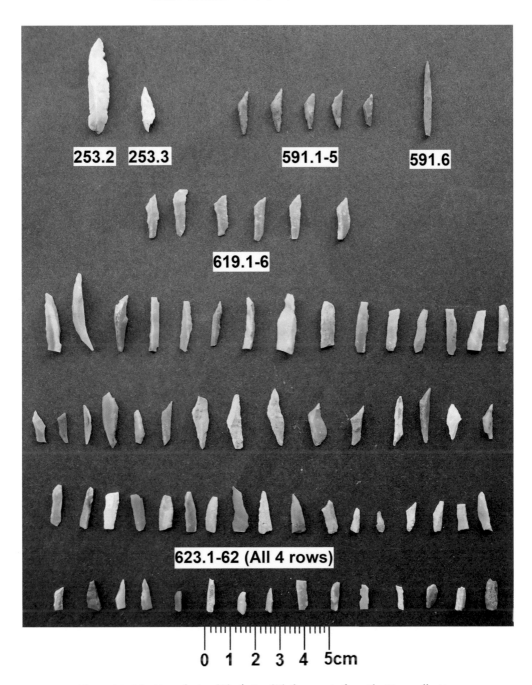

Figure 2.1: Selection of microliths/microlith fragments from the Heys collection

H253.2–3   31–40: Long Plain Farm
H591. 1–5   163: Snilesworth Moor
H619.1–6   176: Urra Moor
H623.1–62   181: Bilsdale E Moor
rod microlith:
H591.6   163: Snilesworth Moor

Figure 2.2: Selection of arrowheads from the Heys collection

barbed-and-tanged arrowheads:
Sutton B type
H54.3   10–29: Dialstone Farm
Sutton C type:
H259.1   31–40: Long Plain Farm
Conygar Hill type
H56.1   10–29: Dialstone Farm
H594.1   163: Snilesworth Moor
H746.1   328: Broomhead Moor
H771.1   339: Salmonby
Kilmarnock type
H500.1   108: Waterloo Farm
oblique arrowheads:
H143.7   10–29: Dialstone Farm
H272.1   31–40: Long Plain Farm

H276.1   31–40: Long Plain Farm
H315.3   41–62: Murton
H699.1   244?: Blubberhouses Moor
transverse arrowheads:
H54.1   10–29: Dialstone Farm
H56.2   "
H166.2   "
H348.1   41–62: Murton
H748.1   328: Broomhead Moor
leaf-shaped arrowheads:
H51.1   10–29: Dialstone Farm
H51.2   "
H207.1   "
H344.1   41–62: Murton
H596.1   165: Arnsgill Ridge, Snilesworth Moor

Figure 2.3: Selection (mostly knives) from the Heys collection

H52.3	plano-convex knife	10–29: Dialstone Farm
H129.1	kite-shaped arrowhead	″
H136.1	kite/leaf-shaped arrowhead	″
H176.1	worked flake/knife?	″
H404.1	worked blade/plano-convex knife?	76–82: Pond Farm
H488.1	knife	95–107: High Lodge Farm
H498.1	kite-shaped arrowhead/spearhead	108: Waterloo Farm
H508.1	denticulate knife/blade	112–13: Studford Farm
H509.1	plano-convex knife/awl	″
H515.1	plano-convex knife (notched?)	″
H538.1	leaf-shaped arrowhead/spearhead (broken)	127–35: High Lions Lodge

Figure 2.4: Selection (axeheads and knives) from the Heys collection

H53.1	axehead fragment (butt end)	10–29: Dialstone Farm
H53.2	plano-convex knife	"
H98.1	axehead	"
H284.1	edge-polished knife	31–40: Long Plain Farm
H287.4	Gp VI ground axehead fragment	41–62: Murton
H294.1	polished axehead (blade fragment)	"
H417.1	axehead	76–82: Pond Farm
H433.2	axehead	87–92: Cold Cam Farm

Figure 2.5: Selection from the Heys collection

H363A.1 discoidal knife/scraper	41–62: Murton
H284A.2 worked flake/scraper	31–40: Long Plain Farm
H284A.1 ground/polished axehead	"
H672A.1 V-perforated jet button roughout	10–29: Dialstone Farm
H284A.5 thumb scraper	31–40: Long Plain Farm
H781.1 black obsidian tool fragment	Easter Island
H491A.1 leaf-shaped arrowhead	95–107: High Lodge Farm
H462A.1 Iron Age/Romano-British glass bead	"
H363A.2 worked flake/arrowhead (fragment)?	1–62: Murton

Figure 2.6: Selection from the Heys collection

H24.1	*whipped cord 'maggot'-decorated Food Vessel (?) sherd*	*10–29: Dialstone Farm*
H77.1	*chevron-decorated Food Vessel (?) rim sherd*	*"*
H77.2	*chevron-decorated Food Vessel (?) sherd*	*"*
H232.1	*'slug' knife*	*"*
H289.3	*metal tag*	*41–62: Murton*
H394.1	*spindle whorl*	*74–5: Scawton*
H348.2	*glass bead (fragment)*	*41–62: Murton*
H497.4	*Jasperware? sherd*	*108: Waterloo Farm*
H555.1	*awl*	*142–3: Givendale Head Farm*
H598.1	*discoidal scraper*	*165: Arnsgill Ridge, Snilesworth Moor*
H778.1	*gun flint*	*345: Brandon, Suffolk*

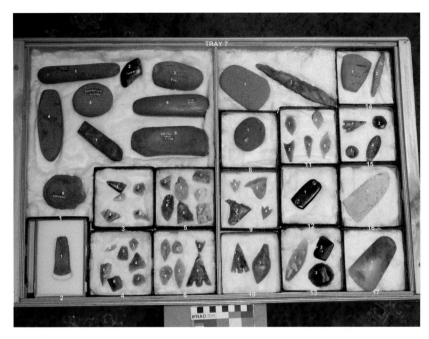

Figure 2.7: Selection from the Taylor collection (Taylor Database 2: Tray7) (Example of one of the twelve trays of artefacts in the Taylor collection)

1.1–9	assorted hammerstones/hones	10–29: Dialstone Farm; 179: Money Howe 93–4: S of Cold Cam Farm
2.1	bronze axehead	188: Bransdale Ridge
3.1–5	assorted arrowheads	20: Hut Field, Dialstone Farm
4.1–7	assorted arrowheads, microlith, blade/gun flint	"
5.1–7	axehead fragment, flakes, slug knife, transverse arrowhead	"
6.1–2, 4–5	leaf-shaped arrowheads	"
6.3	Sutton B barbed-and-tanged arrowhead	"
6.6	Green Low barbed-and-tanged arrowhead	"
7.1–2	sandstone axehead, 'strike-a-light'	"
8.1	hammerstone	unknown
9.1,4	Sutton B barbed-and-tanged arrowheads	168: Cow Ridge; 188: Bransdale Ridge
9.2–3	transverse arrowheads	"
10.1	Conygar Hill barbed-and-tanged arrowhead	168: Cow Ridge
10.2	leaf-shaped arrowhead	"
11.1–2, 4–5	leaf-shaped arrowheads	165: Arnsgill Ridge, Snilesworth Moor; 168: Cow Ridge
11.3	oblique arrowhead	"
12.1	jet wrist-guard (bracer)	20: Hut Field, Dialstone Farm
13.1–3	plano-convex knife	23: Car Park Field, Dialstone Farm
	V-perforated jet button (broken), scraper	26: Jet Buckle Field, Dialstone Farm
14.1–2	ground Gp VI axehead, 'strike-a-light'	106: Long Field, High Lodge Farm
15.1–3	barbed-and-tanged arrowhead, scrapers	247: Rivock, Rombalds Moor
15.4	leaf-shaped arrowhead	unknown
16.1	axehead/knife	"
17.1	polished Gp VI axehead	93–4: S of Cold Cam Farm

Figure 2.8: Selection from the Taylor collection (168: E of Cow Ridge, near Parci Gill, Bilsdale W Moor)

T6.260.11–12   *retouched blades*
T6.260.13   *burin (terminal fragment)*
T6.260.14   *peppery furrow shell (Scrobicularia plana)*
T6.260.15–17   *microliths*
T6.260.18   *Conygar Hill barbed and-tanged arrowhead*
T6.260.19   *arrowhead (distal fragment)*

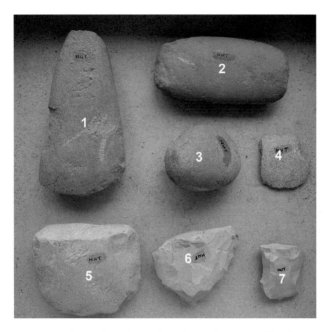

Figure 2.9: Selection from the Taylor collection (20: Hut Field, Dialstone Farm)

T1.20A.1   Gp VI axehead (scratched to reveal original colour)
T1.20A.2,3   hammerstones
T1.20A.4   ground/polished Gp VI axehead flake
T1.20A.5   ground/polished Gp VI axe (butt fragment)
T1.20A.6–7   Gp VI axehead roughout fragments

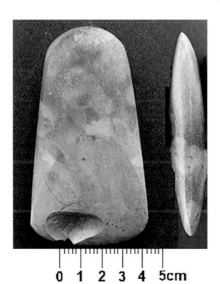

Figure 2.10: Polished Gp VI axehead
(T2.7.17.1) (93–4: S of Cold Cam Farm)

Figure 2.11: Selection from the Taylor collection (23: Car Park Field, Dialstone Farm)
T4.9A.1–6,8–11,13–14   *cores*
T4.9A.7,12   *cores?*
T4.9A.15,16   *'strike-a-lights' (formerly termed 'fabricators')*

Figure 2.12: Selection from the Taylor collection (168: E of Cow Ridge, near Parci Gill, Bilsdale W Moor)

T6.260.1	*flint nodule (flakes removed?)*
T6.260.2–5,7	*cores*
T6.260.6	*worked flake*
T6.260.8,9	*scrapers*
T6.260.10	*worked flake/plano-convex knife?*

Figure 2.13: Taylor collection (244: Round Hill, Blubberhouses Moor) (T18.32.1-18)

1-3	*leaf-shaped arrowheads*
4	*leaf-shaped arrowhead (distal fragment)*
5	*leaf-shaped arrowhead (fragment)*
6	*oblique arrowhead*
7-10	*barbed-and-tanged arrowheads*
11	*barbed-and-tanged arrowhead (longitudinal fragment)*
12-14	*transverse arrowheads*
15	*transverse arrowhead (distal fragment?)*
16	*knife fragment?*
17	*arrowhead/point*
18	*sherd*

Figure 2.14: Selection from the Taylor and Heys collections (348: Langdale Pikes, Cumbria)

1:	T21.38.1	*Group VI axehead roughout*
2–7:	H885.1-6	*Group VI axehead roughouts*

Figure 2.15: (Left:) Lower Palaeolithic hand-axe (T18.97.1) (Wanstead Gravel Pit, July 1899)
Figure 2.16: (Right:) Lower Palaeolithic hand-axe and fragments (H886.1-6) (Barton-on-Sea, Hants.)

Chapter 3:
Featured Artefacts and Artefact Groups

Apart from the sheer size and diversity of the two collections, which alone make them significant, there are a number of notable items or sets of items that merit further detailed discussion and it is to these that we now turn. Again (as in Chapter 2 above) the number and location of each piece is given.

Discoidal knives (Keith Boughey and Alison Sheridan)

'Polished discoidal flint knives' were first recognised, described and illustrated as a distinct group of artefacts by Sir John Evans in his seminal volume on stone implements published in the 19th century (Evans 1872: 292–310), and were later the subject of an extensive study by Clark (Clark 1929) based largely on examples in existing museum and private collections in South-East England, London and Scotland. According to Clark, they could be divided on the basis of their shape into roughly circular (Type I), triangular (Type II), lozengiform or leaf-shaped (Type III), and rectangular (Type IV). A recent piece of unpublished PhD research by Melissa Metzger examining their typology and subjecting them to use-wear analysis, has refined Clark's long-established classification, recognising an additional sub-type to Type IV, 'polished edge discoidal knives' (Metzger 2018). Dating from the Late Neolithic, they are distinguished from the far commoner plano-convex knives not only by their polish but also by being slightly convex on *both* sides, and bifacially worked around the *entire* perimeter to provide a continuous cutting edge, unlike a horseshoe scraper which has a flat 'base' and is only worked on the upper convex side around part of the perimeter to provide a scraping as opposed to a cutting edge. This and the sheer skill that clearly went into the production of discoidal knives make them objects to admire.

Clark's original study described 133 examples recovered mainly from sites in South-East England and Norfolk, but relatively few from Yorkshire, most of which (13) were from the Yorkshire Wolds, as well as one from the coast near Whitby and one from Harome in the Vale of Pickering, though this last example, first illustrated and described by Evans, was not in fact made of flint (Evans 1892: 343 fig. 259; Clark 1929: 45 note 4). Although the number of known examples has since almost doubled, they remain relatively low in number compared to other classes of flint artefact, and little was known of their depositional or cultural context until research for a PhD by Julie Gardiner, based on a detailed study of finds across the South Downs, drew a number of tentative conclusions for at least one part of the UK (Gardiner 2008). However, according to Gardiner, depositional information is available for two of examples from the Wolds, both of Clark's rectangular Type IV, excavated by Mortimer: one from Aldro (Mortimer 1905: 74 Barrow No. C75, Plate XIX fig. 160), and the other from a burial at Duggleby Howe (Mortimer 1905: 28 Barrow No. 273, Plate VII fig. 58). The latter is associated with a radiocarbon date, obtained by Alex Bayliss and Alex Gibson for the associated human remains, of 4344±33 BP (OxA-16747), which was calibrated (using OxCal v3.10) and Bayesian modelled to 2980–2885 cal BC (95.4% probability) (Gibson et al. 2009: table 1). Again, the list of Taylor-Heys discoidal examples (Figs.3.1–3.5) is dominated by Dialstone Farm and the arable fields in the south and west as opposed to the open moorlands of the central region to the north, as evident from Table 3.1 below. Unfortunately, as with so many examples, they were all surface finds lacking in any specific depositional or datable context.

Table 3.1: Discoidal knives (in order of lithic no)

Lithic No.	Description	Location
H42.1	discoidal knife/scraper	10-29: Dialstone Farm
H127.1	discoidal knife	"
H127.2	discoidal knife	"
H275.1	semi-discoidal knife	31-40: Long Plain Farm
H363A.1	discoidal knife	41-62: Murton
H499.2	discoidal knife/scraper fragment	108: Waterloo Farm
H598.1	discoidal scraper	165: Arnsgill Ridge, Snilesworth Moor
T1.272.1	discoidal knife	91: White Barrow Field, Cold Cam Farm
T2.10.5.5	discoidal knife	23: Car Park Field, Dialstone Farm
T3.90.4	ground/polished discoidal knife fragment?	60: White Barrow Field, Murton
T3.251.1	discoidal knife fragments (re-assembled)	168: Cow Ridge, Bilsdale W Moor
T6.280.6	discoidal knife fragment	"

Discoidal knives are much less common than most other forms of knife, but by no means unknown. Of only 18 discoidal knives recorded on the Portable Antiquities Database (at the time of writing: March 2022), not one is from Yorkshire. Of 51 examples in the British Museum collections, just five are from the county: one marked simply 'Yorkshire' in the Wollaston Franks collection acquired from Lord Londesborough in 1888 but almost certainly from an unspecified location somewhere in East Yorkshire (BM: +3997), and a second from Huntow near Bempton (BM: Sturge 454), which might be the same one mentioned by Evans in 1897 as then being in the Greenwell collection (Evans 1897: 341–2). Among the thousands of flint items recorded in the vast Greenwell collection now in the British Museum, only three further discoidal knives are known, all from Yorkshire, though none from the North York Moors. The first is a fragment recovered from an unspecified location during the excavation of Round Barrow XXIX at Ganton on the edge of the Wolds (BM: 1879, 1209.332a) (Kinnes and Longworth 1985: 43, illustrated); the second is a complete knife found in the mound of one of the many round barrows dug into at Rudston (Rudston LXVII) (BM: 1879, 1209.1011) (Kinnes and Longworth 1985: 75, illustrated); and the third comes from a round barrow at Bishop Burton (Bishop Burton CCLXV Littlewood XI) (BM: 1879, 1209.1638) (Kinnes and Longworth 1985: 124, illustrated). However, all three are 'cruder', smaller examples than those in the

Figure 3.1: Discoidal knife (H598.1) (165: Arnsgill Ridge, Snilesworth Moor)   Figure 3.2: Discoidal knife (T1.272.1) (91: White Barrow Field, Cold Cam Farm)

Taylor and Heys collections (Figs. 3.1–3.5), averaging 4.5–5cm in diameter and only roughly circular. The Yorkshire Museum collections list ten flint discoidal knives, though sadly all lacking precise provenance though presumably from the county: six are simply listed as from 'York' (and un-illustrated) (YORYM : FW 100.1; YORYM : FW 100.2; YORYM : FW 100.5; YORYM : FW 1006.; YORYM : FW 100.8; YORYM : FW 100.43), three even more poorly provenanced as being merely from the 'UK' (YORYM : 2001.5170-2) (Figs. 3.6–3.8), and one from just 'North Yorkshire' (YOYRM : 5039) (Figure 3.9).

More recently, at least in the second half of the 20th century, Cowling reported and illustrated two unassociated finds of discoidal knives in the county: one from the well-known Late Neolithic/Early Bronze Age location of Green Crag Slack on the northern edge of Ilkley Moor in mid-Wharfedale, and the second from Fylingdales Moor (https://www.Pastscape. org.uk: Monument No. 29815), both of which were more oval than circular, with a small dip in the perimeter of the shorter axis that Cowling interpreted as an incurving handgrip (Cowling 1963). The Green Crag Slack knife was the larger, 8.0cm (across 'handgrip') x 9.3cm wide, comparable in size to one in the Taylor collection (T1.272.1) (Figure 3.2), and the one from Fylingdales Moor, 5.4cm (across 'handgrip') x 7.0cm wide. There is no sign of any such 'handgrip' on any of the Taylor-Heys examples; these show a closely circular profile. A third example, again from the North York Moors, is an oval discoidal knife/scraper, measuring 7.0cm x 4.5cm, found in 1958 a ploughed field near north of Shepherd's House near Baysdale Beck at NZ 629074 (https://www.pastscape.org.uk: Monument No.: 28042), reported and illustrated by Hayes (Hayes 1964). Manby lists 43 examples of polished flint knives and scrapers in Yorkshire, of

Figure 3.3: Selection of discoidal knives from the Heys collection
(H127.1-2 10-29: Dialstone Farm)
(H275.1 (fragment) 31-40: Long Plain Farm)

Figure 3.4: Discoidal knife (H363A.1)
(41-62: Murton)

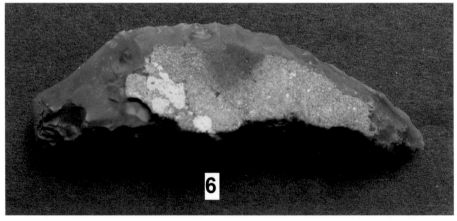

Figure 3.5: Discoidal knife fragment (T6.280.6) (168: Cow Ridge N, Bilsdale W Moor)

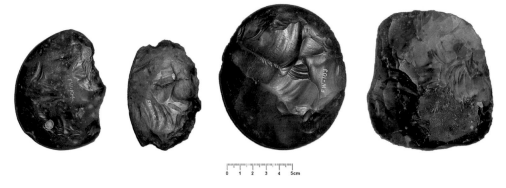

Figures 3.6–3.8: (Left) Discoidal knives 'from the UK' (Yorkshire Museum YORYM : 5170–2)
(© YMT, CC BY-SA 4.0)
Figure 3.9: (Right) Discoidal knife 'from North Yorkshire' (Yorkshire Museum YORYM : 5039)
(© YMT, CC BY-SA 4.0)

which ten – including the aforementioned Baysdale Beck knife – come from the North Riding (Manby 1974: appendix 1). However, given their comparative rarity in the overall flint record, especially those that are circular or near circular, it is of some significance that two further examples have been reported from Kepwick alongside the 'Cleveland Road' track at a point just 3km north (SE 409 919) of the northern edge of Taylor's and Heys' collecting area at High Paradise (Mackay 1979).

Tess Durden identified Late Neolithic production sites for this artefact type on the Yorkshire Wolds (Durden 1995), and it may be that, to some extent, the products of the specialist flintworkers on the Wolds were made for export. This is consistent with Torben Ballin's finding that many items of Yorkshire flint, including discoidal knives, ended up in southern Scotland (Ballin 2011: 61). Discoidal flint knives are also known to have been produced during the Late Neolithic (more specifically, between *c.* 2725 and 2400 BC) at Grimes Graves in East Anglia (Healy *et al.* 2018). Well-dated examples of polished discoidal knives from anywhere in their distribution area are extremely scarce, but, as noted above, one sub-rectangular all-over-polished example associated with the unburnt remains of a man (burial D) at Duggleby Howe is radiocarbon dated, from the man's bone, to 2980–2885 cal BC (95.4% probability) (Gibson *et al.* 2009).

Arran pitchstone

This solitary small pear-shaped worked flake of Arran pitchstone (Figure 3.10), measuring 21.8mm long x 14.8mm wide x 5.0mm thick, complete with a characteristic bulb of percussion on its ventral face and conchoidal scars on the dorsal face, was found in the plough soil of the 'Car Park Field' (SE 5120 8530) at Dialstone Farm. At first sight, it might seem to be something of an oddity, maybe even mistaken. But Alison Sheridan and her colleagues at the National Museums

Figure 3.10: Worked flake of Arran pitchstone (T2.10.18.2) (23: Car Park Field, Dialstone Farm) (© J.A. Sheridan)

of Scotland (NMS) have confirmed the identification and regard it as a rare Neolithic example of Arran pitchstone this far south and well worthy of publication. According to Torben Ballin, an expert in the dating and distribution of Arran pitchstone in the prehistoric period (Ballin 2008; 2009; 2015a; 2015b), worked pieces of the material have been found as far from Arran as Barrow in Furness, the Isle of Man, and Lambay Island north-east of Dublin. To the north of Arran there are finds from various sites in Scotland, with Orkney being the northernmost findspot (Figure 3.11).

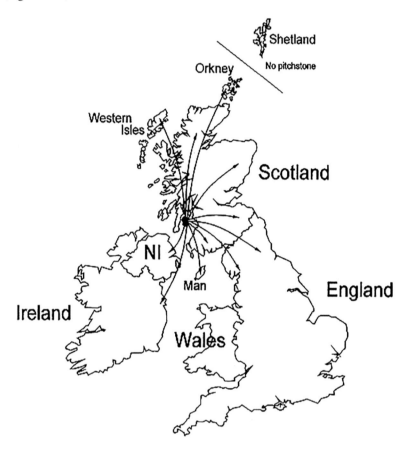

Figure 3.11: Distribution of Arran pitchstone across northern Britain (after Ballin 2015a) (© Creative Commons Licence, courtesy of T.B. Ballin)

The problem in England is that there are so many pitchstone 'look-alike' types of material, such as fine-grained black chert, black flint, jet, coal, glassy slag, smoky quartz, etc. that many potential pieces have therefore probably been missed by those unfamiliar with pitchstone (Wilson-Thorpe and Thorpe 1984; Ballin 2009). The presently available radiocarbon dates relating to pitchstone use in Scotland confirm that it was first used during the Mesolithic period (on Arran, with exchange of rare individual pieces in central Scotland), and during the Early Neolithic (around 3800–3500 BC) it was exchanged systematically throughout northern Britain; it is during this period that the flake reached Yorkshire.

Haematite

Haematite, principal component iron(III) (ferric) oxide, Fe_2O_3, is a common mineral still prized today in jewellery for its fine appearance when polished. Its blood-red colour accounts for its name (Greek: *haima* blood). Red ochre, a naturally occurring combination of haematite and clay, is a much-prized pigment with a long attested use throughout prehistory.

Figure 3.12: Haematite 'rubber' (T2.7.1.2) (23: Car Park Field, Dialstone Farm) two views

The Taylor collection contains six pieces, two of which at least show signs of use: T2.5.16.1 (polished) and T2.7.1.2, a small fragment of black haematite (Figure 3.12). Quarter-ovoid and wedge-shaped in plan and with a single rounded end, it measures 52.8mm x 28.8mm x 29.5mm, and according to Sheridan is smoothed and gently faceted through use as a prehistoric 'rubber'. When rubbed against a hard surface, black haematite leaves a distinctive red-brown streak (as used for example to decorate the wall of the Neolithic 'Structure 1' at the Ness of Brodgar) (https://en.m.wikipedia.org/wiki/Ness_of_Brodgar; Card *et al.* 2020) or to decorate pottery. Both pieces come from the 'Car Park Field' (23: SE 5120 8530) at Dialstone Farm. As a matter of remarkable recent coincidence, an example of a unique red ochre crayon in the UK was reported from a site on the shore of the former palaeo-lake Flixton in the Vale of Pickering. The site consisted of a mixture of Late Upper Palaeolithic and Early Mesolithic lithic scatters, and small quantities of animal bone although the authors believed that a Mesolithic association was more likely (Needham *et al.* 2018). The source of the red ochre is likely to have been Cumbria, where the mineral is still mined today (e.g. at Egmont), raising the question of whether or not it was traded in the same way as other valuable commodities in the Early Bronze Age period such as flint, jet and amber.

Bronze axehead/axehead ingot

Curiously, and perhaps due not so much to their inherent rarity but to the corrosive nature of much of the soil on the North York Moors, there are very few 'copper alloy' (i.e. bronze) items to report, all from the Taylor collection. Of the seven items recorded, all but one of them are very probably fragments of relatively modern pieces, possibly made of brass and not bronze, and represent casual losses in the field or on the moor. The one remaining is a remarkably well-preserved complete Early Bronze Age small, flat axehead (or possibly axehead ingot) with a slightly flared blade, length 58mm, maximum width (at blade) 27mm, found on Bransdale Ridge, Bilsdale E Moor, at SE 615 915 approx. (T2.7.2.1) (Figure 3.13). It shows no obvious signs of wear or damage, and its unusually small, almost miniature size, raises the possibility that this was not in fact a finished axehead but an 'axehead ingot' ready for heating and pouring into a mould. With possible affinities to the Migdale metalworking tradition, it could date from *c.* 2200–1950 BC (Needham 2004).

The best-known *comparandum*, though noticeably broader and more concave-sided, is the Butterwick type axehead recovered by Greenwell from the eponymous Early Bronze Age barrow (Greenwell XXXIX) in East Yorkshire (Kinnes and Longworth 1985: 45), along with a Series 2(A) bronze dagger (Needham 2015, 23), dated to 2100–1900 BC and a set of jet, jet-like and stone buttons (Sheridan 2015a: 167–9). But the nearest *comparanda* are two Early Bronze Age Migdale type flat axeheads from the southern half of the region (Elgee 1930: 78). The first, from Lockton, (Figure 3.14), is in the Greenwell collection at the British Museum (BM: WG.1794) and was illustrated by Elgee (Elgee 1930: plate X fig. 2). The second, found at Scackleton in Ryedale, is in the Mortimer collection held by Hull Museum (Radley 1974: 17). A full list of all the bronze items in the Taylor collection is given in Table 3.2 below.

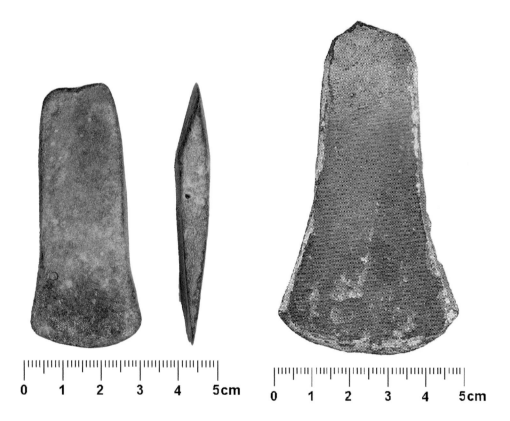

Figure 3.13: Bronze axehead/axehead ingot (T2.7.2.1) (188: Bransdale Ridge, Bilsdale E Moor) (front and side views) (© R. Banens)

Figure 3.14: Bronze axehead, Lockton (from Elgee 1930, plate X fig. 2)

Table 3.2: Bronze/copper alloy artefacts

Lithic No.	Description	Location
T1.258.9	brass ring	47/51: Arrowheads Field, Murton
T2.3.5.3	brass hinged scale?	23: Car Park Field, Dialstone Farm
T2.7.2.1	bronze axehead	188: Bransdale Ridge
T3.120.4	brass button?	66: Coronation Farm, Cold Kirby
T3.120.5	brass spoon?	"
T3.189.3	dot-decorated ring fragment	130: Long Field, High Lions Lodge
T3.202.4	strap fitting?	138: Beacon House Farm, Ampleforth

Coins

A small number of coins, mostly Victorian, were occasionally picked up from the ploughed fields: the most notable exceptions being two Roman coins (Figure 3.15), an Edward I (1272–1307) silver penny (Figure 3. 16 and see Figure 3.17) and two silver coins from the reign of William III and Mary II (1689–1702, but postdating the death of Mary in 1694) (Figure 3.18). Full details are given below in Table 3.3.

Table 3.3: Coins

Lithic no.	Description	Location
T1.291.2	Victorian halfpenny	29: No. 1 Field, High Barn Farm
T1.136.19	George V 1923 halfpenny	12: Cemetery Field, Dialstone Farm
T1.55.21	1d penny	20: Hut Field, Dialstone Farm
T1.55.22	½d halfpenny	"
T1.108.14	Victoria 1859 silver threepence?	"
T1.130.12	Victoria 1861 halfpenny	"
T1.162.15	Victoria halfpenny?	"
T1.62A.6	Victoria halfpenny?	25: Plantation Field, Dialstone Farm
T1.170.3	Victoria 1861 halfpenny	29: opposite Hut Field, Dialstone Farm
T1.228A.1	Roman silver denarius Maximinus I (AD 235–8)	40: Valley Field, Long Plain Farm
T1.247.1	Victoria 1863 penny	138: Beacon House Farm, Ampleforth
T1.210.13	Victoria halfpenny	unknown
T2.4.3.3	William III (1689–1702) silver sixpence/love token	22: Car Park Field Bank, Dialstone Farm
T2.6.17.4	Victoria 1860 penny	23: Car Park Field, Dialstone Farm

Lithic no.	Description	Location
T2.10.7.5	William III (1689–1702) silver shilling	"
T2.6.12.2	George V 1931 silver shilling	109-11: Far Moor Park, Westwood Rigg
T3.5.1	Edward I (1272–1307) silver penny	1: Field 4, High Paradise Farm
T3.183.1	Roman silver denarius Vespasian (AD 69–79)	120: Roman Coin Field, Stiltons Farm

The finding of the silver denarius of Vespasian from the eponymously named 'Roman Coin Field' at Stiltons Farm in the Vale of Pickering on the southern edge of the North York Moors is possibly not without significance. Vespasian became Emperor after the death of Nero following on from his successful subjugation of southern Britain before command of the Roman army in Britain passed to his successor Agricola. It was Agricola who continued the campaign in the north, including in territory occupied by the Brigantes in what is now more or less Yorkshire. If nothing else, and allowing for whatever may have been the coin's period of currency, as some coins continued to be used long after they were first issued, this find at least provides evidence for an early Roman presence in the area.

Although badly damaged by the plough, the second Roman coin, this time from the similarly eponymously named 'Silver Coin Field', Long Plain Farm, on the western edge of the North York Moors, can be identified as a silver denarius from the reign of the Emperor Maximinus I (AD 235-8). The obverse of the coin (Figure 3.15) clearly shows the emperor's distinctive profile of pointed chin and beard, wearing a simple laurel leaf diadem, and a distinctive tassel of ribbon tied at the back of his neck. The surviving inscription that can just about be made out is 'IMP MAXIMINUS PIUS (AUGUSTU)S'.

Figure 3.15: Roman silver denarius Maximinus I (AD 235-8) (T1.228A.1) (40: Silver Coin Field, Long Plain Farm) (image digitally enhanced by the author)

Although it is unwise to base too much on the find of a single coin, this later 3rd century coin nevertheless adds to a growing body of evidence for both military and domestic Roman activity in the region. especially across the northern edge of the Vale of Pickering in a band stretching from Beadlam, where there was a Roman villa whose main period of occupation was from the third to fourth centuries AD (Stead 1971; Neal 1996), to Thornton-le Dale, though finds on the moors proper to the north are understandably scarce (Spratt 1993: 156 fig. 70; Wilson 1995).

The silver penny from the reign of Edward I (1272–1307) was picked up as an occasional find from one of the ploughed fields at High Paradise on the western edge of the moors.

Although the coin is heavily damaged by both the ravages of time and the plough, parts of the inscriptions can still just be made out (Figure 3.16). On the obverse of the coin, the lettering would have been one of the many versions in abbreviated Latin of the title 'Edward King of England Lord of Ireland' (such as 'EDW REX ANGL DNS HYB') (Figure 5.17) though the king's face curiously appears to have been (deliberately?) scratched out. On the inverse the letters for London, 'LONDINIENSIS' or 'CIVITAS LONDON', indicate where it was minted.

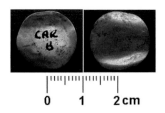

| Figure 3.16: Edward I silver penny (T3.5.1) (1: Field 4, High Paradise Farm) | Figure 3.17: Edward I silver penny (London mint) (© Portable Antiquities Scheme CC BY 2.0) | Figure 3.18: William III silver sixpence/ love token (T2.4.3.3) (22: Car Park Field Bank, Dialstone Farm) |

The rather unprepossessing dented piece of metal shown in Figure 3.18, described by Taylor himself in his diary as a simple 'silver disc' (Diary 21.09.91), when submitted for examination by Adam Parker, Assistant Curator at the Yorkshire Museum, surprisingly turned out to be

Figure 3.19: William III silver sixpence (© Portable Antiquities Scheme CC BY 2.0)

an example of a William III silver sixpence (Figure 3.19), refashioned by smoothing (which has obliterated any of the original insignia) and twisting into an S-shaped love token or good-luck charm (based on the alleged apotropaic properties of silver). When used as a love token, a young man would give one to his intended sweetheart, and if she accepted it, this indicated that she reciprocated his feelings. If she threw it away, this would send the opposite message! Coincidentally, the museum itself has an almost identical example recorded on the Portable Antiquities Scheme Database (PAS YORYM-D88E1E) found in Bridlington in 2019. The Latin inscription '[GVLIELMVS] III DEI GRA' (as in Figure 3. 19) can still just about be made out on the obverse of the heavily worn coin.

Glass

Next is a selection of glass objects and fragments from the two collections, mostly from the Late Victorian period (or possibly so: Figure 3.21) but including a number of notable prehistoric pieces too (Table 3.4, Figs. 3.20, 3.22–3.25). Of particular interest are a number of dark blue annular beads, each based on such a similar lobed quasi-floral design (Figure

3.21) that they could almost be thought to constitute a matching set and to have come from the same necklace, and significantly all found in the same field at Dialstone Farm, though at different times. But these are easily surpassed by the superb Romano-British glass bangle fragments from Beacon House Farm near Ampleforth (T1.247.2) (Figs. 3.22–3.23) and from Dialstone Farm (T2.10.16.3) (Figs. 3.24–3.25). Also of interest is a plano-convex glass counter (H415.1, not illustrated), probably a playing piece and probably of medieval date. It measures 27.25mm in diameter and 7.1mm in thickness, and it has a slightly eccentric hollow that had been a socket for an inlay: two tiny hollows within the socket exist to pin the inlay in place, and there is a tiny chip of what may be amber – an orange material, at least – in the hollow. This may be the last trace of an inlay. The area around the socket has superficial scratches.

Table 3.4: Glass artefacts

Lithic no.	Description	Location
H348.2	aqua glass bead (fragment)	41-62: Murton
H415.1	semi-perforated glass button	76–82: Pond Farm
H462A.1	Romano-British perforated turquoise glass bead	95–107: High Lodge Farm
T1.43.9	Victorian? dark blue 13-lobed annular glass bead	20: Hut Field, Dialstone Farm
T1.139.6	Victorian? dark blue 4-lobed annular glass bead	"
T1.150.10	Victorian? dark blue 5-lobed annular glass bead	"
T1.150.11	Victorian? dark blue annular glass bead	"
T1.172.24	Victorian black glass decorated fragment	12: Cemetery Field, Dialstone Farm
T1.247.2	Romano-British multi-stranded glass bangle fragment	138: Beacon House Farm, Ampleforth
T2.10.16.3	Romano-British multi-stranded glass bangle fragment	23: Car Park Field, Dialstone Farm
T3.117.2	Late Victorian imitation jet floral manganese dioxide tinted black glass brooch fragment	?: opposite Murton
T3.128.9	glass/rock crystal bead	76–82: Pond Farm
T3.184.2	Romano-British glass bead	120: Roman Coin Field, Stiltons Farm

Figure 3.20: Romano-British (?) plain glass bead (fragment) (H348.2) (41-62: Murton)

Figure 3.21: Victorian? annular glass bead (T1.43.9) (20: Hut Field, Dialstone Farm) (© R. Banens)

Figure 3.22: Romano-British glass bangle fragment (T1.247.2) (138: Beacon House Farm, Ampleforth) (© R. Banens)

Figure 3.23: Extrapolated inner diameter (T1.247.2) (© R. Banens/K. Boughey)

The first and smaller of two glass bangle fragments dating to the Romano-British period (Figure 3.22) was found at Beacon House Farm (NGR SE 597 793 approx.), 1.5km east of Ampleforth at the foot of the North York Moors in the Vale of Pickering. Made of olive-green glass, it carries two cords of blackish-brown and white glass. The fragment measures 37.5mm x 7.5mm x 9.5mm. Assuming the bangle to have been circular, the estimated inner diameter is around 60mm and the outer diameter 71mm (Figure 3.23). Romano-British bangles occur in three size groups: those with an interior diameter of 40–45mm (which might not have been used as bangles at all); those with an interior diameter of 55–65mm could have been worn on women's lower arms (as confirmed by experimental work by Tatiana Ivleva); while those whose inner diameter ranges between 70mm and 90mm were probably worn on women's upper arms (Ivleva 2018).

Found by Taylor at Dialstone Farm in the so-called 'Car Park Field' (NGR SE 5120 8530), easily one of the most prolific of all the locations he visited, is this second and larger fragment of a Romano-British glass bangle (Figure 3.24). It measures 44.2mm (outer length) x 14.2mm thick x 9.4mm wide, and again assuming the complete bangle to have been circular, its estimated inner diameter is around 82.5mm and external diameter around 106mm (Figure 3.25). It is beautifully made of a translucent pale blue glass with three inlaid twisted cables of red, white and blue glass and an applied central cord of blue and white glass, creating a series of chevrons.

According to Dr Fraser Hunter, Principal Curator of Later Prehistoric and Roman Archaeology, National Museums Scotland, both are examples of what is known as a Kilbride Type 2 bangle after the typology established by Howard Kilbride-Jones in 1938 (Kilbride-Jones 1938). This typology was refined in 1988 by Jennifer Price (Price 1988), so we are able to say that the Beacon House Farm example is a Type 2Ai, while the Dialstone Farm example is a Type 2Bi; the presence of an inlaid cord on the side of the hoop is unusual. Fashionable in the earlier period of Roman occupation, glass bangles are common across the north of England, with a particular concentration of finds in the north-east, in what would then have been Parisi territory (Price 1988; Ivleva 2018; Paynter et al. 2022). A manufacturing site has been identified at Thearne, East Yorkshire (Paynter et al. 2022). The date range for Romano-British glass bangles in the

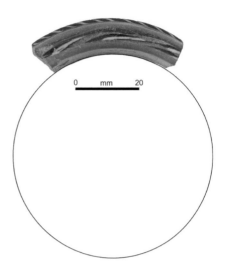

Figure 3.24: Romano-British glass bangle fragment (T2.10.16.3) (23: Car Park Field, Dialstone Farm) (© J.A. Sheridan)

Figure 3.25: Extrapolated inner diameter (T2.10.16.3) (© J.A. Sheridan/K. Boughey)

north of Britain is the late first to the mid-2nd century AD; their use in Britain had died out before the turn of the 3rd century when bangles of jet and similar-looking materials rose in popularity (Allason-Jones 2011: 2; Ivleva 2018; Paynter *et al.* 2022: 16). Once assumed to be high status objects, bangles were not the preserve of the elite in Romano-British society, but were worn across the social spectrum (Ivleva 2018).

Remarkably similar examples can be found recorded on the Portable Antiquities Scheme Database from Sneaton, near Whitby (YORYM : 6D12A7) and in the East Riding of Yorkshire, from Bainton (YORYM : 620A34), Kilham (YORYM : B985BA), Rudston (YORYM : 7325B6), Burton Fleming (YORYM : 6EC79C) and Roos (FAKL : C8D895). No fewer than five Romano-British glass bangles are currently held in the York Museum Trust's collections. The first (YORYM : 2006.2857), 60mm in diameter and 7mm thick and from York, is made from dark blue glass with a ridged deltoid profile (Figure 3.26). A cord runs round the outside, featuring white, dark and opaque yellow glass. Both the upper and lower edges are highlighted with white lines. The second bangle (YORYM : HG5), 49mm in diameter and 7mm thick and again simply described as from York, is made from green glass, ridged and deltoid in section, with a cord around the ridge in an irregular blue and white pattern (Figure 3.27). Regrettably, two of the remaining three, all of similar design and workmanship, have no provenance details and are not illustrated on the YM collections web-site (https://www.yorkmuseumstrust.org.uk/collections). The first (YORYM : 22.6193), from an unidentified excavation but presumably either from York, or at least the county, is a 22mm fragment of blue-green glass with two cords of interweaving blue and white glass running around the outside (Figure 3.28); the second (YORYM : 2013.1337), of unknown dimensions, is again a fragment of blue-green glass with a blue and white twisted circumferential cord but with additional bands of yellow-green and white glass running around both shoulders. The final fragment (YORYM : HG8) is much the same as the first but with additional evidence of two ovate knobs finished off dramatically with strands of swirling black and white glass.

Figure 3.26: Romano-British glass bangle (York Museum Trust: YORYM : 2006. 2857) (© YMT, CC BY-SA 4.0)

Figure 3.27: Romano-British glass bangle (York Museum Trust: YORYM : HG5) (© YMT, CC BY-SA 4.0)

Figure 3.28: Romano-British glass bangle fragment (York Museum Trust: YORYM : 22.6193) (© YMT, CC BY-SA 4.0)

Jet/Jet-like artefacts

(For more detailed descriptions of all of these artefacts, please consult Appendix 2).

The next group of objects to be dealt with in the collections is in some ways perhaps the most remarkable since it includes two exceedingly rare items – a wristguard (bracer), T2.7.12.1, and a probable skeuomorph of an Early Bronze Age belt-hook (T2.7.13.2), both from Dialstone Farm. Jet was a highly prized material in prehistory (especially during the Early Bronze Age) and in its finely polished state was reserved for high status jewellery and dress accessories such as necklaces, bangles, studs and buttons. Early Bronze Age artefacts of jet and of similar-looking materials are widespread in Britain, with examples across England from Northumberland to Dorset (Woodward and Hunter 2015), as well as in Wales (Sheridan and Davis 1998) and Scotland (Sheridan and Davis 2002).

Thanks to a unique set of geological circumstances, the only major source of workable jet in Britain is located on the North York Moors, particularly where it outcrops along the coastline around Whitby. Indeed, the source of the jet is often understandably slightly misquoted in the archaeological and historical literature as 'Whitby jet' as it occurs in localised deposits across the whole of the North York Moors. This is clearly shown on a map drawn up of the award of jet mining contracts across the North York Moors in the Late Victorian period (Figure 3.29), at a time when its exploitation and value surged due to the wearing of jet jewellery by Queen Victoria, following the death of Prince Albert in 1861. Licences were granted to exploit seams and outcrops along the sides of Ryedale, Bilsdale, Bransdale and Rosedale, along the western and north-western scarp edges south of Osmotherley and as far as Kildale, and along the coast from Saltburn to Lythe. Indeed, finds of jet artefacts from Yorkshire dominate the archaeological record (Woodward and Hunter 2015: 136, 149, 261, 286) so it is perhaps not that surprising that items of jet and jet-like material form such a prominent set of artefacts in the Taylor and Heys collections: some 97 pieces, 51 of which are worked.

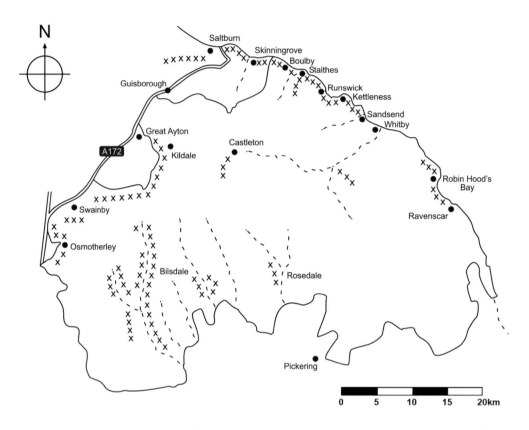

Figure 3.29: Map showing the award of jet mining contracts on the North York Moors (Based on an original by Helen Muller; reproduced courtesy of Rebecca Tucker, W. Hamond Museum of Whitby Jet)

This is not the place to discuss the role of jet in British prehistory – this has already been done more than adequately by Alison Sheridan (e.g. in Woodward and Hunter 2015 *passim*); sufficient here, having set the context, to give a summary of the jet and jet-like pieces in the collections and focus on the more noteworthy objects. A full catalogue, with details kindly provided by Sheridan (for the earlier prehistoric material), Fraser Hunter (for the Iron Age/Romano-British material) and Rebecca Tucker, Curator of the W. Hamond Museum of Whitby Jet in Whitby (for the Late Victorian material), is provided in Appendix 2; this catalogue also details the unworked pieces of jet, and pieces of jetworking debitage of indeterminate date, in the collection. The following summary has been provided by Sheridan, Hunter and Tucker, with the tables compiled by the author.

Neolithic (Alison Sheridan)

Three artefacts are of definite or possible Neolithic date (Table 3.5): two possible examples of an Early to Middle Neolithic type of bead known colloquially as a 'monster bead' (Figs. 3.30–3.31), of which one (Figure 3.31) could have broken during manufacture; and a broken roughout for a Middle Neolithic belt slider (Figure 3.32). All have the characteristic features of jet.

Table 3.5: Jet artefacts – Neolithic

T1.95.7	Early Neolithic 'monster bead'?, incomplete	28: Dialstone: opposite Hut Field
T2.10.19.4	Early Neolithic 'monster bead'? roughout, incomplete	23: Dialstone: Car Park Field
T2.3.11.2	Broken roughout for Middle Neolithic belt slider	"

The fragmentary bead T2.10.19.4 (Figure 3.30), of flattish, sub-circular shape, had broken across its broad perforation and had lost part of one side, while T1.95.7 (Figure 3.31) appears to be a broken roughout for a similarly flattish and similarly sized sub-oval bead; much of its outer surface has spalled off. The closest parallels to these items are Early to Middle Neolithic 'monster beads' – so named because of their chunky appearance – which are widespread, albeit rare, in Britain. Examples have been found not only in jet but also in similar-looking materials such as cannel coal and Kimmeridge shale. Shapes range from elliptical to sub-circular; some have collared ends, and some, like the examples here, are flattish. Around 37 are known, including the two possible examples here. They have been found in Early Neolithic funerary contexts such as the Notgrove Severn-Cotswold long barrow, Gloucestershire, and in domestic contexts, as at Pitlethie Road, Leuchars, Fife (Sheridan 2007b). A necklace comprising a dozen such beads (mostly of jet) plus amber beads, found with a blade-polished flint knife at Greenbrae, Aberdeenshire (Kenworthy 1977), could have come from a grave but this was an old find and insufficient details of the find circumstances exist; nevertheless, both the necklace and the axehead are likely to be imports from Scotland. 'Monster beads' are known from Yorkshire, with one stray find from near Thornborough, North Yorkshire; one found on the old land surface under a round barrow at Painsthorpe Wold barrow 4, East Riding (Mortimer 1905: 116, fig. 275); and one found under a round or long barrow at Maiden's Grave Farm, Bridlington, East Riding (Kinnes and Longworth 1985: 146, UN.103:1). The available dating evidence suggests a currency between *c.* 3800 BC and *c.* 3500 BC, possibly extending

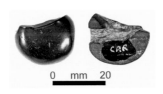

Figure 3.30: Fragment of possible 'monster bead' (T2.10.19.4): exterior surface and (right) fracture surface showing exposed perforation (23: Car Park Field, Dialstone Farm) (©: J.A. Sheridan)

Figure 3.31: Fragment of possible 'monster bead' roughout (T1.95.7): exterior surface and (right) fracture surface showing exposed perforation (28: opposite Hut Field, Dialstone Farm)

a little later; too few are associated (indirectly) with radiocarbon dates for a more precise estimate of their currency to be offered. They would have been precious and prestigious possessions.

Object T2.3.11.2, from the Car Park Field, Dialstone (Figure 3.32) is a fragment of a broken roughout for a belt slider. It had broken along a natural laminar plane and across the pierced part of the object, and the facts that the surviving end still has flake scars from initial roughing out, and that the striations at the edge of the hole have not been ground smooth, point towards this being a roughout that broke during the manufacture process. Its original overall length is likely to have been *c.* 70mm.

These distinctively-shaped artefacts are of Middle Neolithic date and their identification as belt fittings is based on the fact that four have been found at the hip of adult males in graves (at Whitegrounds and Painsthorpe barrow 118, North Yorkshire; Barrow Hills, Radley, Oxfordshire; and Handley Down barrow 26, Dorset: Sheridan 2012). It is unclear whether they had been used as a kind of buckle, attached to one end of a belt with the loose end threaded through them, or else as a means of

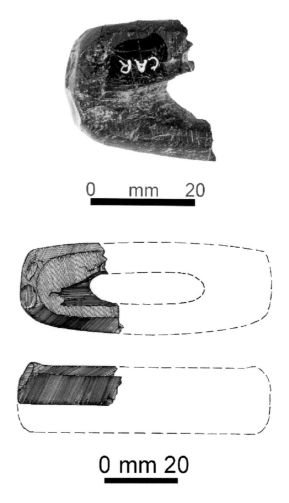

Figure 3.32: Belt slider fragment (T2.3.11.2) (23: Car Park Field, Dialstone Farm) (Photo © J.A. Sheridan; drawing © M. O'Neil)

securing the loose end of a belt, like a loop on modern trousers; if the former, however, then most of the surface of the object would have been obscured while in use, which is at odds with the likelihood that these precious items were made for display, designed to be admired. The sparse evidence for use-wear – consisting of locally-heightened polish to the outer edge of the perforation (Sheridan 2012) – could conceivably support the 'buckle' idea but does not offer a definitive pointer as to how 'sliders' were deployed.

Belt 'sliders' of jet and similar-looking materials are widespread in Britain, being found as far north as Skye and as far south as Cornwall, with concentrations in Yorkshire and along and near the Thames (Sheridan 2012). A review in 2012 listed 29 examples (Sheridan 2012); the Dialstone Farm example constitutes the 30th, and a further example has recently been found at Barrow Clump, Wiltshire (examined by the author in the Wessex Archaeology store). Available radiocarbon dates for associated unburnt human remains indicate a currency between *c.* 3300

BC and *c.* 3000 BC, with the Linch Hill example being associated with a slightly earlier date of 3640–3380 cal BC; a date of 2880–2500 cal BC for the Barrow Hills individual is believed to be anomalously late, derived from relatively poorly preserved bone (Sheridan 2012).

Chalcolithic?/Early Bronze Age (Alison Sheridan)

This category encompasses several types of artefact, namely finished and unfinished V-perforated buttons with round bases; a wristguard (bracer); a trapezoidal, V-perforated object likely to be a belt fitting; a possible belt ring; fusiform and other beads; fragmentary 'napkin rings'; and a fragmentary stud. While most are clearly of Early Bronze Age date (within the overall date range 2200–1500 BC), one cannot altogether rule out the possibility that some of the V-perforated buttons could be of Chalcolithic date (2500–2200 BC), as buttons are known to have been introduced as a novel dress accessory during that period. In addition, there are a couple of objects that could be of Early Bronze Age or of much later, Iron Age date. Bangle fragments, which fall into that category, are dealt with in the 'Iron Age/Romano-British' section below as they are most likely to be of that date, even though bangles of jet-like materials are known to have been in use during the Early Bronze Age.

Many of the jet artefact finds of definite and possible Early Bronze Age date, including roughouts, come from Dialstone Farm which raises the question of whether there could have been a settlement and/or funerary monuments of that date in the area.

V-perforated buttons

Five V-perforated jet buttons with a domed or conical profile and roughly circular base shape are represented among the Taylor-Heys collection: three finished items (H12.2, H435.2 and T3.97.6, Figs. 3.33–3.35) and two roughouts (H672A.1, Figure 3.34, and T2.12.13.3), as follows (Table 3.6):

Table 3.6: V-perforated buttons

H12.2	V-perforated button	1–5: High Paradise
H435.2	small conical V-perforated button	87–92: Cold Cam Farm
H672A.1	roughout for V-perforated button	10–29: Dialstone Farm
T2.12.13.3	roughout for V-perforated button	23: Car Park Field, Dialstone Farm
T3.97.6	V-perforated button	41: Big Field N of crossroads, Murton

While all are most likely to be of Early Bronze Age date, probably dating to between 2200 BC and *c.* 1900 BC (and this is definitely the case for the small conical button from Cold Cam Farm, Figure 3.35), nevertheless it is known that V-perforated buttons began to be used in Britain during the Chalcolithic period (Shepherd 2009), and so a pre-2200 BC date for the High Paradise, Dialstone Farm and Murton examples cannot altogether be ruled out, although it is arguably unlikely.

None of the finished buttons shows signs of heavy use; indeed, the small Cold Cam Farm example (Figure 3.35) retains the grinding striations on its base that relate to its manufacture,

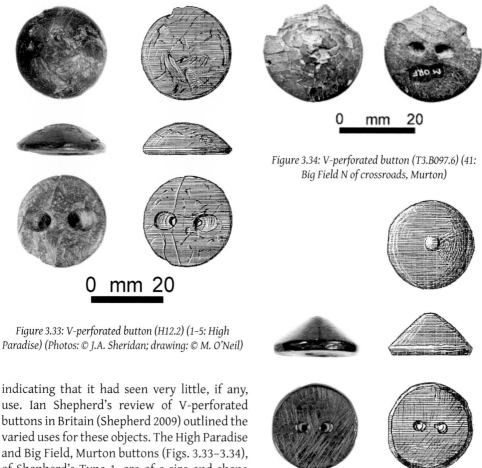

Figure 3.34: V-perforated button (T3.B097.6) (41: Big Field N of crossroads, Murton)

Figure 3.33: V-perforated button (H12.2) (1-5: High Paradise) (Photos: © J.A. Sheridan; drawing: © M. O'Neil)

Figure 3.35: V-perforated button (H435.2) (87–92: Cold Cam Farm) (Photos: © J.A. Sheridan; drawing: © M. O'Neil)

indicating that it had seen very little, if any, use. Ian Shepherd's review of V-perforated buttons in Britain (Shepherd 2009) outlined the varied uses for these objects. The High Paradise and Big Field, Murton buttons (Figs. 3.33–3.34), of Shepherd's Type 1, are of a size and shape comparable to those found in sets (usually of five or six) used to fasten men's jackets (Shepherd 2009; Woodward and Hunter 2015: section 5.3). The smaller example from Cold Cam Farm (Figure 3.35), of Shepherd's Type 2, can be paralleled among a set of 20 found in an adult's grave at Hunmanby, East Yorkshire (Woodward and Hunter 2015: 164–7 and fig. 5.3.3), their position in a row from the neck to the waist again suggesting their deployment as jacket fasteners. Elsewhere, small conical V-perforated buttons may have been used as decorative studs rather than as functioning buttons.

Regarding the two roughouts from Dialstone Farm, item H672A.1 (Figure 3.36) had been destined to be a low-domed button, abandoned before the process of drilling the V-perforation had been completed: a shallow 'starter hole' can be seen to the right of the larger 'starter hole' in Figure 3.36. An unsuccessful attempt had been made to grind smooth a large flake scar on the underside. Grinding striations can clearly be seen all over the lower and upper surfaces.

Figure 3.36: Roughout for a low-domed V-perforated button (H672A.1) (10–29: Dialstone Farm). Note the 'starter' drill-hole marks on the underside (right) (© J.A. Sheridan)

It could be that this roughout was abandoned because the maker realised that it was too shallow to take a V-perforation. As for the other button roughout from Dialstone Farm (T2.12.13.3, Figure 3.37), this was destined to be a small conical button similar to the Cold Cam Farm example, but without the facet around the bottom of the cone. It had broken while the upper surface was being ground, and before any attempt to drill the V-perforation had begun. The presence of button roughouts in the Taylor-Heys collection is significant as they attest to Early Bronze Age jetworking on the western edge of the North York Moors.

Figure 3.37: Broken roughout for small conical V-perforated button (T2.12.13.3) (23: Car Park Field, Dialstone Farm) (© J.A. Sheridan)

Wristguard (bracer) from Hut Field, Dialstone Farm (T2.7.12.1) (20: 'Hut' Field) (Figure 3.38)

This is one of the most significant objects in the Taylor-Heys collection, because only one wristguard of remotely comparable material is known from the whole of Britain and Ireland. Found by Taylor in April 1994 at Dialstone Farm (20: 'Hut' Field SE 5140 8481), it measures 57.0mm x 28.0mm x 8.25mm, and is sub-rectangular in both plan and cross-section and slightly wedge-shaped in longitudinal section, with natural undulations visible in the surface of the jet on both flat sides. The edges have been gently squared off and a few faint vertical grinding striations are visible on the thicker of the two end edges. The two perforations have been drilled from either side, roughly mid-way along the narrow ends and close to the edge; one is oval and measures 4.8mm x 3.7mm in its interior, the other rounder and measures 2.2mm x 2.2mm. At each end, a thread-pull groove extends from both sides of the perforation to the end of the object, indicating that it had seen some wear by the time it was discarded or deposited. The object has been polished to a high sheen all over, except for the thicker of the two ends, which has a low sheen. According to the system of classification devised by Jonathon Smith

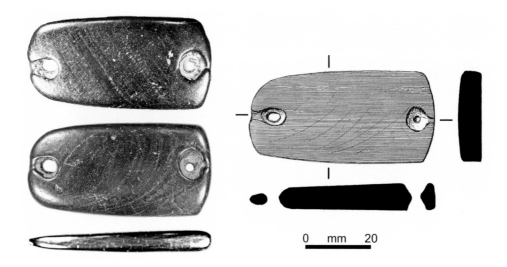

Figure 3.38: Jet wristguard (T2.7.12.1) (20: Hut Field, Dialstone Farm) (Photos: © J.A. Sheridan; drawing: © M. O'Neil)

(Smith 2006), this is an example of the '2SF' type, i.e. 2(-holed), s(traight-sided) and f(lat). Confirmation that the raw material is indeed jet was obtained through compositional analysis using X-ray fluorescence spectrometry, by Dr Lore Troalen of National Museums Scotland.

There is only a single *comparandum* known, from a suspected grave containing a Beaker (of East Anglian type) and a barbed-and-tanged flint arrowhead at Cliffe on the Hoo peninsula in the Medway district of Kent (Figure 3.39; Kinnes and Cook 1998; Woodward and Hunter 2011: 31, 45, 122, 173 [ID 153]; British Museum Reg. No. BM: 1978,1101.1220). The wristguard was found underneath the Beaker, and the raw material has been claimed by Fiona Roe to be 'probably Kimmeridge shale' (Woodward and Hunter 2011: 45; cf. Kinnes and Cook's 'shale') and this would be consistent with Roe's description of the material as 'laminar', although to judge from the photographs taken for the Woodward and Hunter volume, it seems equally if not more likely that the material is jet – and this would tally with the previous life of the artefact, as detailed below. Compositional analysis would be required to check the material identification The surface has been obscured by consolidant. Like the Dialstone Farm example, the Cliffe wristguard has two hourglass-shaped perforations and it is closely comparable in length, although it is narrower: sub-rectangular in shape with rounded ends, it measures 56mm long x 18mm wide x 6mm thick. It has flattish surfaces and gently rounded edges. The underside has multi-directional grinding striations and traces of what appear to be the apex of shallow V-perforations, indicating that this had been reworked from a different kind of artefact. As Kinnes and Cook note, the original object must have been of considerable size; the only plausible candidate would be one of the very large 'cloak fastener' V-perforated buttons, of which an example 81mm in diameter is known from Lynchard in Dorset (Shepherd 2009: 337). As regards the likely date of the Cliffe wristguard, even though several two-holed wristguards are known to be of Chalcolithic date (e.g. Dornoch Nursery: Woodward and Hunter

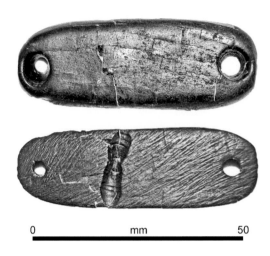

Figure 3.39: Cliffe wristguard; note the remains of the V-perforation on the underside (Photos courtesy of Ann Woodward)

2011: 88, 154), the associated Beaker is of a type that appears to date to *c.* 1950–1700 BC (Needham 2005) and so this is likely to be of Early Bronze Age date, as is the Dialstone Farm example. This is consistent with the Cliffe example having had a previous life as a large V-perforated button.

The function of these objects has been much discussed, with some having argued that they were functioning wristguards, used to protect an archer's wrist from the recoil of a bowstring. However, ever since Fokkens *et al.*'s study of their positioning on the arm of male skeletons (2008) highlighted the fact that many have been found on the *outside* of the arm, rather than on the inside where a wristguard would be needed, it has widely been acknowledged that these so-called 'wristguards' are much more likely to have been ostentatious ornaments, attached to a functioning wristguard of animal hide (e.g. Smith 2006; van der Vaart 2009a; 2009b), than wrist-protectors in their own right. Indeed, had they been worn on the inside of the wrist, they could have caught on the bowstring as it recoiled. They could have been lashed on or riveted on to the outside of a hide wristguard; the pattern of wear on the Dialstone Farm example indicates that it had been lashed on with a thong. The interpretation of such objects as ornaments, like north American silver 'ketoh' wristguard ornaments (Fokkens *et al.* 2008), is consistent with the choice of brittle raw material/s used to make the Dialstone Farm and Cliffe examples: these objects are unlikely to have withstood the pressure of being worn on the inside of the wrist.

Trapezoidal, V-perforated object likely to be a belt fitting, possibly a skeuomorph of the Bush Barrow belt hook (T2.7.13.2) (26: Jet Buckle Field, Dialstone Farm, SE 5106 8627) (Figure 3.40)

Like the wristguard from Dialstone Farm, this is a very significant and rare object, and it has a complex life-history. It is incomplete but would originally have been slightly trapezoidal in shape, with gently squared-off corners, and it would probably have measured around 46mm x 44mm x 6.9mm when complete, as the reconstruction drawing indicates (Figure 3.40). The upper surface is slightly domed and has decoration in the form of triple incised lines running parallel with its outer edges; the underside is flat. It had originally been V-perforated, and one of the sloping perforations survives; the drill had accidentally burst through the upper surface during the drilling process. The object had broken across the V-perforation and along one of its edges in antiquity but it continued to be used after that: it was re-perforated with a vertical hole (drilled from the front and the back) that would have enabled it to be worn as a pendant. It was worn for long enough for the fracture surfaces to be worn smooth. The material has been confirmed as jet through X-ray fluorescence spectrometry undertaken

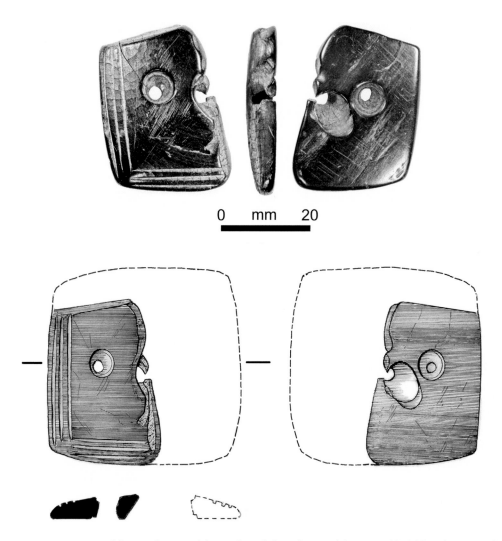

Figure 3.40: Fragment of decorated trapezoidal V-perforated object (T2.7.13.2) (26: Jet Buckle field, Dialstone Farm)
(Photos: © J.A. Sheridan; drawing: © M. O' Neil)

by Dr Lore Troalen of National Museums Scotland. The jet is black and blackish-brown, its variegated colours revealing the original structure of the wood from which the jet had formed.

In its original form, this object will have appeared virtually identical in shape, size and decoration to a trapezoidal V-perforated object of cannel coal found in a cist on The Law, Dundee before 1880 (Figs. 3.41–3.42; Sturrock 1880: figs 8–9; Clarke *et al.* 1985: 208, 283, fig. 5.47). That object measures 43mm x 41.5mm.

Both the Dialstone Farm and Dundee Law objects differ from Early Bronze Age V-perforated buttons in having a distinctly trapezoidal shape, and it is quite possible, if not highly

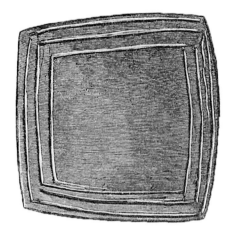

Figure 3.41: V-perforated cannel coal object, probably a belt fitting, from the Law, Dundee (After Sturrock 1880; reproduced with permission of the Society of Antiquaries of Scotland)

Figure 3.42: Photograph of the V-perforated object from The Law, Dundee, orientated at 90° to its probable orientation of use (From Clarke et al. 1985; © National Museums Scotland)

probable, that they had been belt accessories, fixed onto one end of a belt so that the belt could be fastened by looping a cord round the trapezoidal objects, analogous to the 'toggle and loop' fasteners on a modern duffle coat. During the Early Bronze Age, just as during the Middle Neolithic, belts for high-status men were ornamented with ostentatious fittings. Early Bronze Age examples, in jet and jet-like materials, bone and gold, have been reviewed by Sheridan (Sheridan 2007c). It is possible that the trapezoidal shape and the linear decoration of the Dialstone Farm and Dundee Law objects were a deliberate emulation of the exquisite, somewhat larger sheet gold belt hook from the Early Bronze Age barrow at Bush Barrow (Wilsford G5), Wiltshire (Needham et al. 2010) – a kind of skeuomorph, in other words (Figure 3.43). There are several examples of where fashions current in early second millennium Wessex were emulated elsewhere. The date of the Bush Barrow belt hook has been estimated at 1900–1750/1700 BC (Needham et al. 2010).

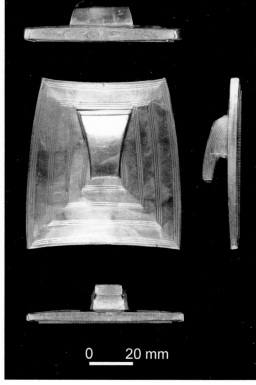

Figure 3.43: Dialstone Farm and Dundee Law trapezoidal V-perforated objects compared with the Bush Barrow gold belt hook. Shown roughly to scale; note that the orientation is at 90º to the probable orientation of use, as the hook would fasten in a horizontal plane (Photographs: Dialstone Farm © J.A. Sheridan; Dundee Law © National Museums Scotland; Bush Barrow © David Bukach/University of Birmingham, reproduced courtesy of Ann Woodward)

Fragment of possible Early Bronze Age belt ring, similar to 'pulley' belt rings – but a later date cannot be ruled out (T2.12.20.5) (23: Car Park Field, Dialstone Farm) (Figure 3.44)

A possible example of a different kind of Early Bronze Age belt fitting – a so-called 'pulley belt ring' – is represented by the fragment of a rectangular-sectioned, perforated jet ring found in Car Park Field on Dialstone Farm (Figure 3.44). Its original external diameter is estimated at *c*. 30mm and part of a transverse perforation can be seen at the fracture surface. This item was initially thought to be a finger ring of Iron Age or Roman date, but the presence of the transverse hole argues against this. The item has a passing resemblance to an Early Bronze Age artefact type known as a 'pulley belt ring', although with these, the perforations tend to be diagonal V-perforations rather than simple transverse perforations. Pulley belt rings would have been attached to the end of a belt, and the loose end of the belt would have been threaded through to fasten it. Since this object lacks the V-perforation seen on Early Bronze Age pulley belt rings, one cannot rule out the possibility that it is of later date. This suspicion is strengthened by Fraser Hunter's observation (pers. comm.) that "There is also a poorly studied group of rings which seems to have opposed perforations through the wall. One comes from Green Castle, Portknockie [in north-east Scotland]...so could well be Late Bronze Age". Clearly more work is needed on the possible comparanda for the Car Park Field find.

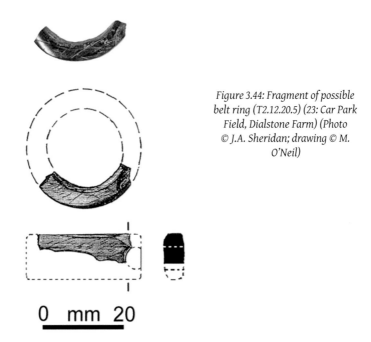

Figure 3.44: Fragment of possible belt ring (T2.12.20.5) (23: Car Park Field, Dialstone Farm) (Photo © J.A. Sheridan; drawing © M. O'Neil)

Fusiform and other beads (and bead roughouts) of definite and possible Early Bronze Age date (Alison Sheridan)

Four beads (or parts thereof), and two bead roughouts, fall into this category, as follows (Table 3.7):

Table 3.7: Beads and bead roughouts of definite and possible Early Bronze Age date

T2.6.8.4	small, slender fusiform bead	23: Car Park Field, Dialstone Farm
T1.239.2	half of plump fusiform bead	125: Arch Field, Duncombe Park
T2.9.4.1	bulbous bead fragment	23: Car Park Field, Dialstone Farm
T2.11.24.2	broken roughout for bulbous bead	"
T2.4.17.2	fragment of long, roughly cylindrical bead	22: Car Park Field Bank, Dialstone Farm
T2.11.21.5	early-stage roughout, possibly for chunky disc bead – Early Bronze Age or later	23: Car Park Field, Dialstone Farm

Two beads are of a shape and size consistent with their use in Early Bronze Age jet spacer-plate necklaces. The small, slender fusiform (barrel-shaped) bead (T2.6.8.4) from Car Park Field, Dialstone Farm, 18mm long, has two flattish sides (Figure 3.45). This indicates that it will have sat immediately below the lower of a pair of spacer plates, its shape allowing a number of beads to be accommodated neatly side-by-side. Traces of bead-on-plate and bead-on-bead wear to the bead's ends show that it had been worn in a necklace.

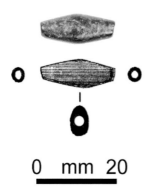

Figure 3.45: Slender fusiform bead (T2.6.8.4) that could have been from an Early Bronze Age jet spacer-plate necklace (23: Car Park Field) (Photo: © J.A. Sheridan; drawing: © M. O'Neil)

The plumper fusiform bead fragment (T1.239.2), found in Arch Field, Duncombe Park, could well have come from elsewhere on a spacer-plate necklace. It is 18.7mm long and had broken along the perforation (Figure 3.46). Spacer-plate necklaces, relatively numerous in Yorkshire where they would have been made by specialist jet-workers, are known to have been made during the Early Bronze Age and used mostly between *c.* 2200 BC and *c.* 1900 BC, although individual components are known to have continued in use later than 1900 BC. (For a detailed discussion of spacer-plate necklaces and their components, see Sheridan 2015b.)

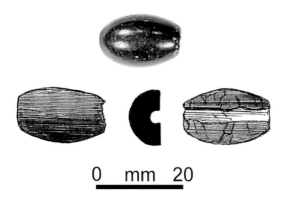

Figure 3.46: Fragment of a plumper fusiform bead (T1.239.2) (125: Arch Field, Duncombe Park) (Photo: © J.A. Sheridan; drawing: © M. O'Neil)

A fragmentary squat, bulbous bead (T2.9.4.1, Figure 3.47) and a broken, final-stage roughout for a bead of similar shape (T2.11.24.2, Figure 3.48), both from Car Park Field, Dialstone Farm, could also be of Early Bronze Age date but probably later than the fusiform beads. Similarly-shaped squat beads of jet and similar-looking materials are known from several necklaces that are likely to date between *c.* 1800/1750 and *c.* 1600 BC (e.g. Fylingdales barrow 271, burial

1, North Yorkshire: Woodward and Hunter 2015: fig. 8.1.3). The roughout bead was at the final stage of manufacture; all that remained, when it broke, was the grinding smooth and polishing of the exterior surface.

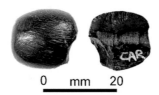

Figure 3.47: Fragmentary squat, bulbous bead (T2.9.4.1) (23: Car Park Field, Dialstone Farm) (© J.A. Sheridan)

Figure 3.48: Broken, final-stage roughout for squat, bulbous bead (T2.11.24) (23: Car Park Field, Dialstone Farm) (© J.A. Sheridan)

Item T2.4.17.2 (Figure 3.49) is half of a long, cylindrical bead from Car Park Field Bank, Dialstone Farm. As with the bulbous beads, parallels can be found in a necklace from Fylingdales barrow 271, burial 1, North Yorkshire (Woodward and Hunter 2015: fig. 8.1.3) and a probable date between *c.* 1800/1750 and *c.* 1600 BC can be suggested.

Figure 3.49: Half of long cylindrical bead (T2.4.17.2) (22: Car Park Field Bank, Dialstone Farm) (© J.A. Sheridan and K. Boughey)

The final item (T2.11.21.5, not illustrated), from Car Park Field, Dialstone Farm, is a small, partly-worked piece of tabular jet, sub-circular in plan and rectangular in section. It is probably an early-stage roughout for a chunky disc bead, for which an Early Bronze Age date is possible, although a later date cannot be ruled out.

Fragmentary dished ear stud

A large part of a large, circular, dished ear stud (T1.208.3) (Figure 3.50) of Early Bronze Age date was found on Turkey Farm. Its outer diameter will have been *c.* 50mm. The inner, knob-like part, which would have been passed through a large hole in the earlobe and would have lain against the neck, had broken off along a laminar plane, and large parts of the circumference had also broken off. The exterior had originally been polished to a high sheen, but its current appearance is dominated by the extensive criss-cross cracking of the jet. There are also traces of a few, short scratch marks on the exterior.

A review of Bronze Age ear studs by Sheridan (in Sheridan *et al.* 2016) catalogued 60 examples from Britain and Ireland, and presented a typology; according to this, the Turkey Farm example can be attributed to her Type 1a, which is among the earliest (if not the earliest) type, probably dating to the early second millennium. Five other Type 1a studs are known, all from North Yorkshire and all made of jet: one from a ring-cairn at Thornton-in-Craven (Sheridan *et al.* 2016: table 16.2, no. 50; Boughey 2015: 81–2); a pair from a barrow at Crossliff(e) (Sheridan *et al.* 2016: table 16.2, nos. 53, 54); and a pair from under the centre of a round barrow at Nawton (Pinderdale Wood, Beadlam: Sheridan *et al.* 2016: nos. 57, 58). While none of these has been dated, their association with round barrows and a ring-cairn strongly points towards an Early Bronze Age date. When worn, these large dished studs would have been very striking in appearance. Several years' worth of earlobe hole stretching would have been necessary to accommodate them. Their similarity and their restricted distribution in North Yorkshire suggest that they could, theoretically, all have been made by the same jetworker or 'workshop'.

*Figure 3.50: Inner face, side, and outer face of large dished ear stud (T1.208.3)
(11: Turkey Farm, Dialstone Farm) (© J.A. Sheridan)*

Fragments of Early to Middle Bronze Age 'napkin ring' garment fasteners

Fragments of two distinctively-shaped annular objects with a concave hoop, known as 'napkin rings' owing to their resemblance to these modern items, are present in the collection (Table 3.8).

Table 3.8: 'Napkin ring' fragments

T1.187.10	'napkin ring' fragment	25: Plantation Field, Dialstone Farm
T1.221.2	'napkin ring' fragments	4: Urn Field, Boltby

The Plantation Field fragment (T1.187.10) (Figure 3.51) constitutes just under a third of the original object, broken both across its circumference and across its body; its external diameter when complete is estimated at *c.* 50mm. It had been polished to a high sheen on both its inner and outer surfaces. The three smaller fragments (plus crumbs) from Boltby Urn Field (T1.221.2) (Figure 3.52) are from a smaller object, with an estimated external diameter of *c.*35mm. While the inner surface has been polished to a high sheen, the exterior is slightly rough and not so highly polished. Both are black, and while they have not been analysed, both could be of jet, especially given the conchoidal fracture surfaces seen on one edge of the Plantation Farm fragment. Future verification of the raw material through non-destructive analysis is recommended.

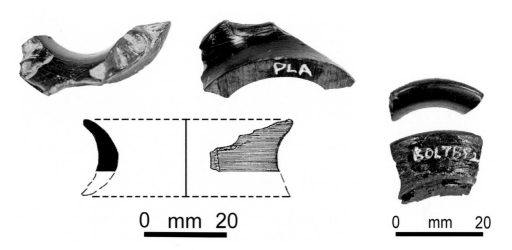

Figure 3.51: Fragment of 'napkin ring' (T1.187.10) (25: Plantation Field, Dialstone Farm) (Photos: © J.A. Sheridan; drawing: Marion O'Neil)

Figure 3.52: Fragment of 'napkin ring' (T1.221.2) (4: Urn Field, Boltby) (© J.A. Sheridan)

'Napkin rings' – which are often wider on one edge than on the other – are a regionally-specific object, being found mostly in southern (and especially south-west) Scotland where almost 50 have been found. Fraser Hunter's 1998 review listed just two examples from England, from Hepburn Moor, Northumberland and from Lockton Pastures, North Yorkshire. Where the Scottish examples have been analysed, they have been found to be of cannel coal rather than jet, and there is evidence (in the form of unfinished examples) for their manufacture at Luce Sands in the former county of Wigtownshire; on Shewalton Moor, North Ayrshire; and possibly also on Stevenston Sands, also North Ayrshire (Hunter 1998: 81). The fact that the outer edge of most examples has not been highly polished (if at all) relates to these objects' use, as suggested by the discovery of a pair in a probable grave at Camps Reservoir, South Lanarkshire (Hunter and Ward 2021; Ward 2021). The position of this pair, lying where the collarbone of the presumed occupant of the grave would have been prior to the body's complete decomposition, strongly suggests that they could have served as giant eyelets for fastening an outer garment such as a cloak, with a thong either passing through them or looped around their outer edges. The inner, highly polished, surface would be on view while the outer surface would have been obscured by the garment. Experimental replication of the Camps pair, and their modelling in use, have been documented in the Camps report (Hunter and Ward 2021: pl. 48–9).

The dating of these objects has been discussed by Hunter (1998; 2021), with a past, erroneous attribution to the Early medieval period being due to an ancient, reworked example having been found in hoard of that date at Talnotrie in south-west Scotland (Hunter 1998: 80–81). The Camps pair were found in a cemetery, of which other graves have been radiocarbon-dated to the Early Bronze Age (with dates on birch charcoal ranging between 3610±50 BP, 2140–1780 cal BC, and 3390±60 BP, 1880–1520 cal BC: Ward 2021, Appendix II). An example from a roundhouse at Blairhall Burn may be contemporary with the use of that roundhouse around 1880–1530 cal BC. A Middle Bronze Age date is suggested for the example found in a house at Blackford, Aberdeenshire (Hunter 2021); dates relating to that house range between 1370–1123 cal BC and 1309–1091 cal BC (O'Connell and Anderson 2021, 35). One cannot rule out the possibility that the 'napkin ring' there was ancient when deposited; alternatively, these items may simply have had a long currency.

Before leaving 'napkin rings', it should be noted that there is a fragment of an object in the Taylor Collection (T2.4.1.1) from Car Park Field, Dialstone Farm that, in its concave shape, offers a superficial parallel for napkin rings (Figure 3.53). With an estimated diameter of *c.* 50mm and wall thickness of 5.25mm, it is deeply scored on its outer edge; the grey-brown material is hard to identify. It is suspected that, rather than being a Bronze Age object, this is of more recent manufacture, and unconnected with 'napkin rings'.

Figure 3.53: Striated, concave object of unidentified non-jet material that is probably not Bronze Age and is not a 'napkin ring' fragment (T2.4.1.1) (23: Car Park Field, Dialstone Farm) (© J.A. Sheridan)

Annular objects probably of Bronze Age date (though an Iron Age date cannot be ruled out) (Alison Sheridan)

Three artefacts from the Taylor collection fall into this category (Table 3.9; Figs. 3.54–3.56). One (T21.37.1) was found by Ronnie Pollard, a workmate of Taylor's who occasionally accompanied him onto the moors, on 26th September 1992, in Car Park Field, Dialstone Farm, and while the Diary confirms the visit and Pollard's presence, it makes no mention of the find (Diary 3, p. 72).

Table 3.9: Annular objects

T1.75.3	complete annular object	20: Hut Field, Dialstone Farm
T2.11.13.2	fragment of highly polished, irregularly annular object	unknown
T21.37.1	complete annular object	23: Car Park Field, Dialstone Farm

It is possible that all three objects, which all appear to be of jet, had been chunky beads or pendants, although the slight flattening of part of the circumference of T21.37.1 and the band of thong(?)-wear on the interior of the hoop at this point (Figure 3.56) suggest that this object had been tightly fixed to something. The fact that all three objects were stray finds means that their dating has to rely on comparison with similar items from elsewhere.

Chunky annular beads/pendants of jet and similar-looking materials are known from Early Bronze Age contexts in northern England, with Woodward and Hunter illustrating several examples from Yorkshire and Derbyshire in their review of Early Bronze Age grave goods (2015, fig. 4.14.2). Of these, the example from Nawton, North Yorkshire – similar in shape to T1.75.3 (Figure 3.54) but a little thinner – provides the most secure stratigraphic evidence for an Early Bronze Age date, having been associated with three jet studs and five fusiform beads in the grave of a probable female aged *c.* 14 years covered by a round barrow (2015: 137, ID 450). That said, Late Bronze Age *comparanda* for T1.75.3 can be cited (e.g. from High Throston, Co. Durham: Brück and Davies 2018: 20–1), and Iron Age *comparanda* for such a simple-shaped object could no doubt also be found, and so it is safest to attribute this to an 'Early Bronze Age to Iron Age' date range.

Figure 3.54: Annular object (T1.75.3) (20: Hut Field, Dialstone Farm) (© J.A. Sheridan)

The asymmetrical bulbous, wedge shape of T2.11.13.2 (Figure 3.55) resembles that of some Late Bronze Age beads that have been found accompanying amber beads in necklaces in northern Britain (e.g. Balmashanner, Angus: Anderson 1892; Henderson *et al.* forthcoming; see also Brück and Davies 2018, fig. 1.12 for an isolated example of such a bead). A recently-found example from the Must Farm Late Bronze Age settlement (discussed by Sheridan in Henderson *et al.* forthcoming) provides a reliable date bracket of 1000–800 BC for such beads. However, as with T1.75.3, one cannot rule out the possibility of an Iron Age date for this chunky bead or pendant.

Figure 3.55: Fragment of highly polished, irregularly annular object (T2.11.13.2) (unknown location) (note: the item is so shiny that the original photographic scale is reflected on its surface) (© J.A. Sheridan)

0   mm   20

Item T21.37.1 (Figure 3.56) is interesting for its clear pattern of wear and its shaping of the circumference, suggesting that it had been secured tightly to something by a thong. There are Late Bronze Age examples of chunky, sub- annular items with signs of wear (e.g. from Llangwyllog, Wales: Lynch 1991; Sheridan and Davis 1998), and the suspicion is that these may have been used in horse harness, although the Llangwyllog examples differ from T21.37.1 in having more pronounced hollows in their circumference and also having lateral perforations through the hoop, so they are not a close *comparandum* for T21.37.1. Once again, possible Iron Age *comparanda* need to be considered, with one chunky annular item found in a grave at Cumledge, Scottish Borders being radiocarbon-dated (from its associated human remains) to 90 BC–AD 30 (Calder 1950; Sheridan 2004).

Figure 3.56: Annular object with thong-wear (T21.37.1) (23: Car Park Field, Dialstone Farm)

0   mm   20

Items that are likely to date to the Late Iron Age/Romano-British period
(Fraser Hunter and Alison Sheridan)

This category encompasses fragments of bangles, plus a disc cut from the centre of a bangle roughout; a finger-ring fragment; and a disc cut from the centre of a roughout for an annular object between a ring and a bangle in size. (See above for other items that might be of Iron Age date). All appear to be of jet. The attribution of a Late Iron Age/Romano-British date to these items can only be provisional, however, as the artefact types (particularly bangles) are known to have been used in Britain at other times as well.

Bangle fragments and core from a bangle roughout

Six bangle fragments, all undecorated, of various hoop shapes (Table 3.10) and with estimated internal bangle diameters ranging from *c.* 56mm to *c.* 85mm, were found (Figs. 3.57–3.58). Of these, two have been perforated, as a way of extending the life of the bangles after they had broken (Figs. 3.57, 3.58 left): broken but conjoining fragments would be perforated and re-attached to each other by means of metal rivets and plates. Indeed, the circular depression seen near the hole on the inside of fragment T1.151.8 may have been caused by the addition of one such joint-plate. One bangle fragment (T1.130.17) has deep transverse cut-marks across the interior of its hoop – a feature that may relate to its process of manufacture (Figure 3.58, right). In addition, one disc that is likely to be a core from the manufacture of a bangle (T1.153.2) was found at Cave Field, Dialstone Farm (not illustrated).

Table 3.10: Bangle fragments and bangle roughout core

T1.24.20	bangle fragment, sub-rectangular hoop	20: Hut Field, Dialstone Farm
T1.124.15	bangle fragment, slender D section hoop	"
T1.130.17	bangle fragment, triangular section, with deep cut-marks across interior	"
T1.135.8	bangle fragment, asymmetric pointed oval hoop section	"
T1.151.8	bangle fragment, subrectangular hoop, perforated, with shallow circular depression on interior around the hole	"
T1.153.2	core from bangle roughout	13: Cave Field, Dialstone Farm
T1.247.3	bangle fragment, probably slender flattish D-section hoop	137: Lupton

Bangles of dark-coloured materials are known to have been used in Britain at various times in the past, from as early as the Early Bronze Age – as attested, for example, by the exceptional Beaker-associated grooved shale bangle from Stanwick, Northamptonshire (Bradley with Edwards 2011) and by debitage from the manufacture of shale bangles and rings at Swine Sty, Derbyshire (Machin and Beswick 1975; see also Needham 2000 for a round-up of Early Bronze Age bangles of dark-coloured materials) – through to the early medieval period (e.g. in south-west Scotland: Hunter 2016). Early Bronze Age examples are rare, however. Large, and also relatively rare, Late Bronze Age examples are known from several parts of Britain (e.g. Carnoustie, Angus: https://guard-archaeology.co.uk/carnoustieHoard/?m=201810; see also

Brück and Davies 2018 on Late Bronze Age objects of jet and similar-looking materials). The peak period of bangle popularity post-dates the Bronze Age, however, and spans the Iron Age to early medieval period. On balance, and in view of the abundance of Iron Age and Romano-British bangles found in northern England, it is most likely that the fragments in Taylor's collection, and the core, belong to this time range (i.e. late first millennium BC to the second quarter of the first millennium AD).

There are two ways of manufacturing a bangle of jet and other dark-coloured materials: perforation of a roughout, followed by expansion of the hole; vs. the cutting out of a circular disc, either by hand or (from the Roman period) with the aid of a lathe. Perforation appears to be the technique used prior to the Iron Age, and it remained the preferred technique in Iron Age Scotland even though elsewhere in the European Iron Age, disc-cutting was used (Hunter 2007; 2016). It may be that the transverse grooves noted in T1.130.17 relate to the final enlargement of the hole. The use of a lathe in bangle manufacture is attested from Roman finds in Yorkshire and elsewhere, where two holes were made in the roughout to accommodate the lathe chuck pegs (Allason-Jones 1996: 11; cf. Denford 2000 on the Kimmeridge shale industry). The absence of such holes in the T1.153.2 core indicate that in this case, the core cutting was done by hand.

It is known that in northern England, the popularity of bangles of jet and similar-looking materials rose from around the turn of the 3rd century AD, superseding glass bangles, whose use had waned from around the middle of the 2nd century AD (Allason-Jones 2011; Paynter *et al.* 2022: 16). While some Roman jet bangles are elaborately carved, most are plain (Allason-Jones 1996: 29–36). Allason-Jones (Allason-Jones 1996: 29) has noted that, by the third and fourth centuries AD in the north-west provinces of the Roman Empire, bangles were almost exclusively worn by women.

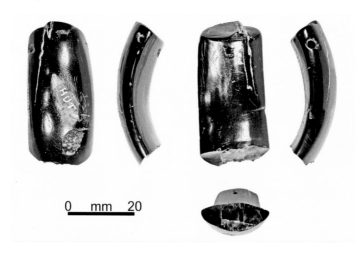

Figure 3.57: Example of a bangle fragment (T1.135.8) (20: Hut Field, Dialstone Farm). Three small holes had been drilled beside one end, but of these, only the central one passes through the hoop; the others are incomplete (© J.A. Sheridan)

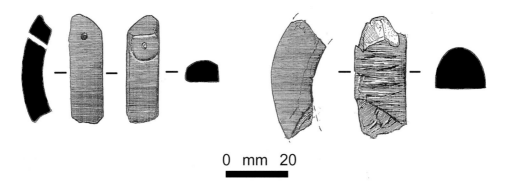

0 mm 20

Figure 3.58: Left: Perforated bangle fragment (T1.151.8); right: Bangle fragment with cut marks on interior of hoop (T1.130.17) (20: Hut Field, Dialstone Farm) (©: Marion O'Neil)

Fragment of finger ring, and core from the roughout of an item intermediate in size between a finger ring and a bangle

The Taylor collection includes one fragment of a jet finger ring plus a core from the roughout of an annular object intermediate in size between a finger ring and a bangle (Table 3.11).

Table 3.11: Finger ring fragment and core from the roughout of an annular object

T2.12.19.9	finger ring fragment	23: Car Park Field, Dialstone Farm
T1.111.10	disc-core from manufacture of an annular object	12: Cemetery Field, Dialstone Farm

The finger ring fragment (T2.12.19.9, Figure 3.59) comes from a ring *c.* 20mm in its external diameter and *c.* 16mm in its interior diameter. It is of simple form, with a hoop of squashed-oval shape. That it had been made by cutting a core from the centre of a roughout by hand is clear from the shallow circumferential scratch mark around its interior and by 'orange peel' surface hollows, the latter resulting from the use of a knife to shape the interior of the hoop. Jet finger-rings were worn by men and women in Roman Britain (Allason-Jones 1996: 37) and a Roman date is possible for this example (even though it has not been lathe-turned), but an earlier date during the Iron Age, or indeed a later date in the early medieval period, is also possible.

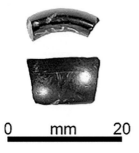

Figure 3.59: Fragment of finger ring (T2.12.19.9) (23: Car Park Field, Dialstone Farm) (© J.A. Sheridan)

0 mm 20

The disc-core (T1.111.10, Figure 3.60) has a diameter of *c.* 37mm, making it too large to have been from a finger ring roughout and too small to have been from a bangle roughout. It has been cut from a roughout block, and the apparent re-working of its outer edge suggest that it could have been used after it broke. Lindsay Allason-Jones (1996: 35) has discussed Roman, lathe-turned annular objects of comparable size, suggesting possible uses ranging from teething rings for children to belt dividers or symbolic bangle substitutes. Non-Roman, Late Iron Age annular objects of comparable size are also known – for example at Castle Law, Angus, where the external diameter of the hoop is *c.* 45mm (Callander 1916: fig. 8), and their function is similarly unclear; some have suggested that they could have been ornaments for the tails of ponies, and while this may seem far-fetched, some connection with horse gear is conceivable.

Figure 3.60: Core from the manufacture of an annular object (T1.111.10) (12: Cemetery Field, Dialstone Farm) (© J.A. Sheridan)

Late Victorian and modern artefacts of jet and substitute materials

(Rebecca Tucker and Keith Boughey, with contributions by Alison Sheridan)

Various materials were used as substitutes for jet in Late Victorian Britain, including cattle horn that was dyed black and moulded (pressed) into shape. Four items made of this material were found on Dialstone Farm (Table 3.12). Two (T1.104.27–8, Figure 3.61) are thin, slightly curving, flat-backed fragments decorated with a foliate design; they could well both belong a single object. They appear too thin to have been from a bangle, but they could conceivably have been parts of a comb. Item T2.2.9.1 (Figure 3.62), of dyed pressed horn, is probably part of a bar brooch, measuring 41.35 x 15.6 x 7.4 (narrowing to 3.2mm where the underside has been hollowed to accommodate a pin. It is decorated with an ogee-ended cartouche featuring a woman's head in profile against a dotted background, with some foliage. Black glass was another jet substitute; this is represented in a fragment of a brooch in the shape of a flower (T3.B7117.2, Figure 3.63). Only one Late Victorian object is actually of jet: a filed fragment that could be a roughout for a bar brooch.

Table 3.12: Late Victorian artefacts of jet and substitute materials

T1.104.27–8	pressed dyed horn, fragments	21: Hut Field Roadside, Dialstone Farm
T1.220.5	pressed dyed horn, fragment	22: Hut Field Bank, Dialstone Farm
T2.2.9.1	pressed dyed horn, prob. a brooch fragment	23: Car Park Field, Dialstone Farm
T2.6.10.1	jet, filed fragment, unfinished bar brooch?	"
T3.117.2	black glass floral brooch fragment	64–5: opposite Murton, N of Wethercote Lane

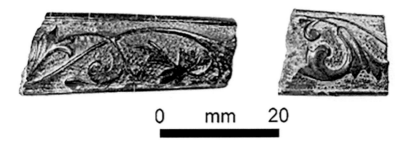

Figure 3.61: Fragments of thin dyed pressed horn plates with foliate design, possibly both from the same object (T1.104.27-8, with 27 on right) (20: Hut Field, Dialstone Farm) (© J.A. Sheridan)

Figure 3.62: Dyed pressed horn brooch fragment with 'Classical' design (T2.2.9.1) (23: Car Park Field, Dialstone Farm) (Photos: © J.A. Sheridan)

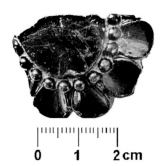

Figure 3.63: Floral black glass brooch fragment (T3.B7117.2) (N of Wethercote Lane, opposite Murton)

Modern

(Keith Boughey)

Included here as it is at least made from jet, this unusual rather crudely carved piece (T3.298.42), curiously reminiscent of a prehistoric arrowhead and to a medieval heraldic harness pendant, though wholly unrelated to such objects (Figure 3.64), was probably intended to be a pendant but was never finished, and significantly is the only jet or jet-like object recovered by Taylor from any of the sites across the higher central plateau. It is assumed to be modern, or at least recent.

Figure 3.64: Modern jet roughout for a pendant or brooch? (T3.B298.42) (171: Bilsdale W Moor)

Jet items of indeterminate date

There are numerous pieces of unworked or partly-worked jet in the Taylor-Heys collection that are impossible to date. These are listed and described in Appendix 2. The partly-worked pieces include roughouts for beads or pendants (e.g. H327.1, H435.1).

Chapter 4:
Excavations

So far the impression might be that the main, if not the sole, contribution made to archaeology by Taylor and Heys was simply what they amassed through their collecting, but they were involved either together or – in Taylor's case, with Jacobi – in five excavations, only one of which, the excavation at Low Paradise, they ever published themselves. Conveniently for the purposes of discussion, as with the collections generally, the excavations belong to two distinct periods and regions: the Early Bronze Age just back from the western scarp edge of the North York Moors, and the Mesolithic on the higher central moorland plateau. These will now be dealt with in turn by region and according to NGR working from west-east and from south-north.

South and West Region (Early Bronze Age Excavations 1–3)

Excavation 1 (Low Paradise Wood, Boltby)

The first excavation to be described, by Heys and Taylor together from February 1992, is of an Early Bronze Age grave above Low Paradise Wood (NGR: SE 5075 8810) and the only one to be published, at least in part (i.e. lacking specific details of the excavation itself and its stratigraphy), but with professional reports on the bone, charcoal, Collared Urn and battle-axehead (Heys and Taylor 1998; Boughey 2019). Taylor subsequently gave the name of 'Boltby Urn Field' (Site 4) to the location of the site, one of the fields belonging to the nearby farm at High Paradise. In a shallow pit packed with stone and earth (Figure 4.1) they unearthed a substantial proportion of the cremated bones and teeth of a young adult male aged between 15 and 25 years of age (T11.9.2–4) within a Secondary Series SE style Form IIIB Collared Urn (Longworth 1984: 27, fig. 17; Manby 1998b) (T11.9.6) (Figs. 4.2–4.3), together with oak charcoal, a few flint flakes and a fine battle-axehead (H4.1) (Figs. 4.4–4.5).

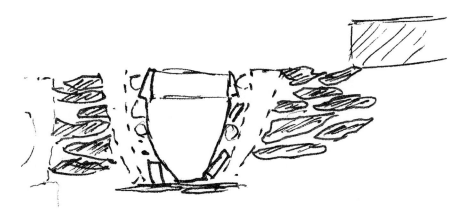

Figure 4.1: Boltby Urn Excavation (drawing in Taylor Diary 3, 37 (23.02.92))

Figures 4.2-4.3: Boltby Collared Urn (T11.9.6) (4: Boltby Urn Field, Low Paradise) (Note the greater height of the urn due to the 'reconstructed' collar in the Manby drawing) (Drawing ©: T.G. Manby)

The charcoal was dated to 3520±50 BP, i.e. 2014–1695 cal BC (Beta-112235). This date compares very favourably with others obtained recently within the county found in direct association with Collared Urns, (Table 4.1) (Boughey 2018) and also compares well with the picture as far north as Scotland where dates mostly cluster within the range 1900–1600 BC (Sheridan 2007a, 163–8). Though not carried out at the time, what would be useful now, given the survival of bone and particularly fragments of teeth, would be to carry out isotope analysis on the cremated bone to look into the likely origins of the cremated individual.

N.B.: Throughout the book, radiocarbon dates have been calibrated using OxCal v.4.4.4 and IntCal 20, and the calibrated dates are cited at 95.4% probability, unless stated otherwise.

The following – hitherto unpublished – is the full account of the discovery and excavation of the site as recorded in Taylor's Diaries. It gives a good impression of how careful and thorough they were both in excavating and recording what they did. Although neither of them had any recognised formal archaeological qualifications, what they achieved – particularly in Taylor's case who had excavated before in the company of Roger Jacobi – was based on solid experience.

'09.02.92 Sun. To Boltby crossroads – first field deep ploughed and weathered – flints found. Second field very recently ploughed and weathered – 3rd field weathered somewhat – very fine powdered surface...On return to 1st field David found a piece of fresh-broken pottery - G.V.T. [i.e. Taylor] trowelled out 3 others – marked area – possible urn site.

Table 4.1: Radiocarbon dates obtained within Yorkshire from material in direct association with Collared Urns

Site	Lab.Ref.	Uncalibrated BP	calibrated BC	Context	Material	Style[1]	Period[2]
Baildon[3]	SUERC-88463	3327±30	1687–1515	cremation pit in centre of barrow	cremated bone	NW	L
Callis Wold 114[4]	GrA-22385	3495±40	1931–1693		cremated bone	NW	M
Cross Farm[5]	OxA-18361	3554±31	2015–1773	cremation pit	cremated bone	NW	M
	SUERC-16360	3555±35	2021–1770	cremation pit	cremated bone	NW	M
Hare Hill (ring cairn)[6]	SUERC-60346	3538±29	2017–1774	cist: base of outer circle inner edge	cremated bone	too few sherds	
	SUERC-60348	3538±29	2017–1774	cist: base of outer circle	cremated bone	NW	M
	SUERC-60358	3434±27	1875–1631	cist below inner circle	charred wood	NW?	M?
Manor Farm[7]	AA-31521	3560±55	2114–1744		hazel charcoal	NW	M
Mitchell Laithes[8]	SUERC-21248	3485±30	1890–1697	rock-cut cremation pit	cremated bone	SE	M
Rossington Grange[9]	Beta-343148	3490±30	1892–1699	cremation pit in centre of barrow	cremated bone	NW	M
	Beta-343149	3520±30	1931–1749	cremation pit: W barrow 'entrance'	cremated bone	NW	M

[1]: i.e. according to Longworth: NW = North-West tradition, SE = South-East tradition (where known) (Longworth 1984)
[2]: i.e. according to Burgess: M = Middle, L = Late (where known) (Burgess 1986) (though this typochronology is not without its problems: see Sheridan 2007, 165)
[3]: Boughey 2020, 98
[4]: Brindley 2007
[5]: Vyner 2008; Richardson and Vyner 2010; Richardson and Vyner 2011
[6]: Boughey 2015, 91
[7]: Burgess 2001, 76; Vyner 2001, 151
[8]: Speed 2010; Boughey 2010, 2
[9]: Roberts and Weston 2016, 29

16.02.92. Sun. Up track to Boltby to first field to dig on site of pottery found last week...No further pottery found in ploughing – area about 3 ft square cleared to plough-sole which was compact – limestone rocks in strata, red area found in NE corner of hole. Further clearance here increased area of redness and black streaks of charcoal seen – area cleared over redness and cleared around limit of colouration – quite restricted, about 20" dia. with slight elongation to NW – very shallow here, only trace on top of rocks of subsoil. Trowelling over reddened area produced black streaks finally showing as narrow black band on SE side – careful work here showed this to be part of decorated rim urn. Working around red area pieces of burnt red rock and charcoal were removed and other parts of urn rim were finally encountered showing that there was an urn present. Removing further reddened material allowed one to penetrate below rim which confirmed the urn to be standing upright – a dia. of 12" (31 cm) – a tight fit for a 20" hole. We had to remove 'soil' from sides of original hole in order to trowel deeper. From original pit came pieces of intense red burnt rock, pieces of charcoal and odd bits of bones. Further down, nearer to base of urn, extreme burnt red pieces of rock jammed tightly round the vessel. The undisturbed soil (bedrock around the urn) was exceedingly difficult to remove even with modern steel tools. One must give credit to tenacity required by Urn people to make original pit-hole – made only just big enough for the urn.

On deepening excavation urn rim pattern seen – rope impressed in vertical parallel lines – under rim could be seen maggot impressions in horizontal bands. Continued trowelling to urn base – red burnt stone packed around urn here – right up against its side (stones on edge). Odd pieces of charcoal – some quite large and small pieces of bone – very little. Urn lifted and place in thin plastic bag, then raised and lowered into fertilizer bag – placed in cardboard box containing a thick tab rug. Appeared well protected and carried over field to car for journey home, travelled well. Although huge cracks were obvious in the urn body and rim, they did not appear to have worsened on the ride.

20.02.92 Thur. With David and Alan [Alan Taylor, his eldest son] to Boltby...To urn site to clear the ground and attempt to find missing neck and rim sherds. Cleared around urn pit for approx. 4 ft – no sign of other parts or clues as to barrow? Construction – trenched 20 ft to South – no signs of a ditch. Odd 2 pieces of urn found – one of shoulder – looked well-worn as though previously removed – also one small sherd which appeared to be actual rim with cord impression and sharply sloping rim. Filled in site and left marker. Further up field near cliff edge, huge dark mark with many rocks and at one spot cremated bone, nearby was an intensely white patinated transverse arrowhead. Area deeply ploughed and intense mass of twitch roots made digging difficult. The removal of a small area of plough-soil revealed (in area of cremated bone) a 2" to 3" layer of darkened and reddened soil containing much charcoal, and below cremated bone further traces of cremated bone within the dark layer, following bone traces there appeared a hole in which bits of bone and charcoal were found spread over about a 3' x 4' oval shaped hole dug below rock subsoil – bones were mainly in upper area of hole to approx. 20" below rock top level, to Southern end was a piece of pottery (broken sherd) nothing else noted – area too difficult to progress without greater amount of time.

23.02.92 Sun. (With David?) – filled in barrow hole of 20.02.92 Walked to field heading to quarry at High Paradise Farm – small hill near drove road – cremated bones seen here and small bits of pottery – ploughing again all twitch and difficult – appeared to have blackened burnt area as other barrow – but not dug. Spent 1 hr' (Diary 3, 34–40).

The Battle-Axehead

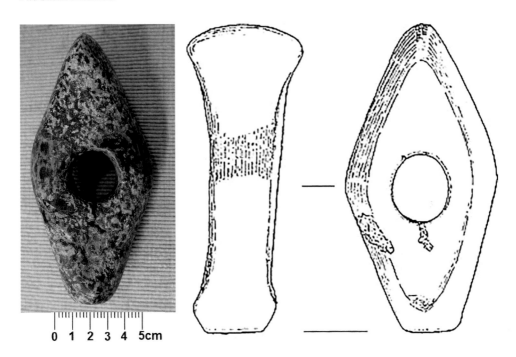

Figure 4.4: Battle-axehead (H4.1) (4: Low Paradise, Boltby)

Figure 4.5: Battle-axehead (H4.1) (4: Low Paradise, Boltby) (as reproduced in Heys and Taylor 1998) (© T.G. Manby)

Dimensions:

Length 132mm, width 67mm, waist 31mm, blade 49mm, butt 39mm, hole (cylindrical, not hour-glass, slightly eccentric, polished around one side) diam. 24mm

According to Manby (Manby 1998c), the Boltby battle-axehead is an example of Roe's Loose Howe Group (Southern Variant) Stage III Butt type D (Roe 1966: 212, fig. 6b). It was examined by Rob Ixer and Vin Davis, who produced a full petrology report (Ixer and Davis 1998). This concluded that the material was best described as an 'appinite', a form of diorite named after the Scottish parish in Western Scotland in which intrusions of the rock were first identified e.g. around Loch Linnhe, Glencoe and the Ardnamurchan peninsula (Johnstone and Mykura 1989) and a Scottish source is suggested as the more likely source. Although appinite outcrops from elsewhere in the British and Channel Isles including the Lake District (http://www. turnstone; Fortey *et al.* 1994), according to Ixer these are small and poorly exposed and with different amphibole composition. Scottish erratics are known from glacial deposits in the eastern areas of England but appinite has not been recognised amongst them. Although an erratic source cannot be excluded it is probably not the most likely origin. The rock has a striking appearance and may have been manuported (Ixer pers. comm.).

Early Bronze Age battle-axeheads were once notoriously difficult to date, partly owing to a lack of association at the time with datable material. In Roe's 1966 metrical survey of 101 examples (even then only around 20% of the known total), fewer than half could be assigned a date on the basis of associated artefacts (Roe 1966: 218–27). Ten of these came from North-East Yorkshire (Roe 1966: table IV; Gilks 1981: 8). However, a sample of oak charcoal from the Boltby burial was radiocarbon dated to 3520±50 BP, 2014–1695 cal BC (Beta-112235). This fits well with two recent radiocarbon dates obtained from cremated bone from a similar Early Bronze Age Type III battle-axehead burial in the county in West Yorkshire, at Cross Farm, Stanbury, west of Haworth, of 3554±31 BP, 2015–1773cal BC (OxA-18362) and 3555±35 BP, 2021–1770 cal BC (SUERC-16360) (Richardson and Vyner 2011), and with the generally agreed range for Type III battle-axeheads of c. 1850–1600 BC based on more recent dating evidence provided by Sheridan (Sheridan 2007a: 175), establishing clear links between the dates of battle-axeheads and their type, thereby supporting the Roe scheme. In what is undoubtedly the best and most comprehensive account of the distribution, typology, petrology, archaeological context and dating of battle-axeheads from Yorkshire produced since, Terry Manby also provides radiocarbon dates from two further Early Bronze Age battle-axehead graves: an 'older', arguably less reliable, larger-range date for human bone from an inhumation associated with a Type III battle-axehead from Wetwang Slack of 3700±70 BP, 2292–1895 cal BC (HAR-4427), and more recently obtained, more reliable dates from cremated remains associated with a Type IV battle-axehead at Low Caythorpe of 3455±30 BP, 1882–1687 cal BC (SUERC-52003) and 3516±27 BP, 1922–1750 cal BC (SUERC-52004) (Manby 2017: 121 table 5.2).

Arguably one of the early problems with battle-axeheads was that of their distinction from axehead-hammers, a distinction first recognised by Ashbee (Ashbee 1960: 107–9). As earlier records show there were 'battle-axes' that were regarded or still are regarded by one source or another as 'axe-hammers', possibly adding to the confusion. However, Roe's meticulous study of both axeheads and axehead-hammers from across the UK cleared up the problem, establishing the distinction between them based on clear criteria, not just of shape (as illustrated for example in Figs. 4.6 and 4.7 below) but of size as well (Roe 1966: 199–203), though she later admitted that there would always be a few marginal examples (Roe 1979: 29–30).

The existence of fragments only serves to compound the problem. The chief weakness of a battle-axehead or axehead-hammer not surprisingly was the perforation designed to take the handle, and this is precisely where a large number of the surviving fragments have broken, leaving one end missing (Manby 2017: 116). If the butt half of the implement is missing, it can be difficult to tell from the surviving tip alone whether the original implement was a battle-axehead or an axehead-hammer or even which of Roe's types to assign it to. This therefore provides an ideal opportunity to revise and augment the list for Yorkshire which originally formed part of Roe's survey (Roe 1966), listing not only those examples which, like the one from Heys' and Taylor's excavation at Boltby, are undisputedly battle-axeheads, but also those examples which have at one time or another been reported as axehead-hammers (Appendix 6).

A comparatively rare find, the Boltby find is one of a series of almost a 100 complete battle-axeheads, plus sizeable fragments, found down the years, many in association with cremated remains in Early Bronze Age Collared Urns, recorded across the county and immediately

Figure 4.6: Battle-axehead
(Hunmanby) (from Evans
1897, 185 fig. 118

Figure 4.7: Axehead-hammer
(Rudston) (from Evans 1897, 195
fig. 127)

adjoining areas (e.g. the Tees valley), mainly recovered from barrows by Mortimer, Greenwell and others from sites in the Wolds and the Vale of Pickering, together with around twenty from the North York Moors (Figure 4.9; Appendix 6). In fact, the nearest find to the Boltby site was a perfect *comparandum* now in the British Museum that was found, according to Spratt, in an Early Bronze Age round barrow on 'Hambleton Moor' (i.e. Hambleton Down), according to his distribution map at NGR SE 5196 8473 a little over 3.5km ESE. However, no such barrow can be located in the literature (Spratt 1993: 106 fig. 43, 148): the nearest being the 'three mounds' allegedly dug into by Tot Lord almost 700m to the south-west at SE 5164 8413 (Figure 1.6: Z). A full list of the details of all battle-axehead finds from the region is given below in Appendix 6.

Wherever it has been possible to establish the sex of the individual associated with a grave, they have invariably been associated with adult males, so it is entirely reasonable to suppose that this was the case at Boltby too. Roe's distribution map of battle-axeheads for the UK (Figure 4.8) clearly shows a number of distinct concentrations, not altogether surprisingly in Wiltshire and the either side of the Thames around London, but also notably the largest concentration is in Yorkshire, particularly across the Vale of Pickering, the Wolds and the southern fringe of the North York Moors, broad enough to include the present Boltby example. Even though this may be partly due to the more favourable chances of recovery given the well-established agricultural nature of the landscape, as pointed put by Manby (Manby 2017: 111), and the patterns of antiquarian collecting activity (e.g. by Mortimer and Greenwell), the concentrations remain significant. As Roe, who made the first recorded serious survey of battle-axeheads across the country and is responsible for both mapping their distribution as well as their accepted typology, herself noted 'The cultural centre, if such it can be called, for battle-axeheads, is in Yorkshire and comparisons can be made with the distributions in this area of Food Vessels...and Primary Series Urns' (Roe 1979: 26), a comment echoed by Manby in his more recent study (Manby 2017: frontispiece).

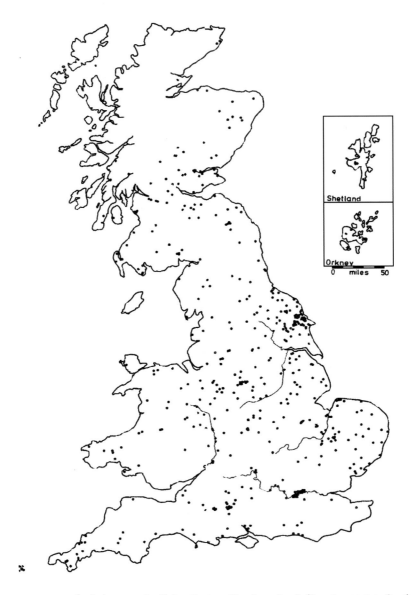

Figure 4.8: UK (excluding N. Ireland) distribution of battle-axeheads (from Roe 1979, 27 fig. 4)
(courtesy of the CBA)

It might be supposed that many – if not most – Early Bronze Age battle-axeheads, especially those recovered from burials, were primarily non-functional ceremonial objects indicative of the deceased's status within the community, traditionally associated with other forms of male weaponry, based on their impressive appearance, fine workmanship, and scant evidence of any actual use or battle damage, though there is no reason in principle why they should not have been both practical as well as ceremonial objects. Now, however, a recently published study (Roy 2020) has cast some doubt on this assumption. Following the results of the first ever large-scale application of use-wear analysis to British Early Bronze Age battle-axeheads

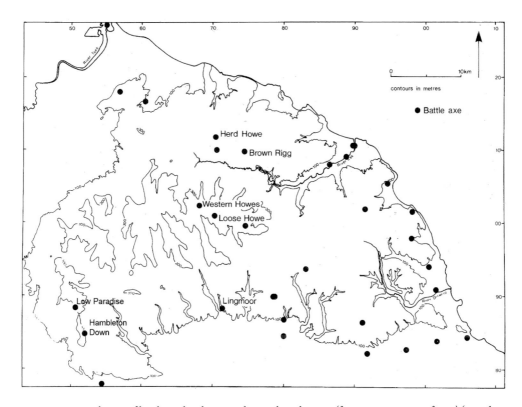

Figure 4.9: Distribution of battle-axeheads across the North York Moors (from Spratt 1993, 106 fig. 43) (note the proximity of the Boltby battle-axehead from Low Paradise to that from Hambleton Down) (courtesy of the CBA)

and axehead-hammers anywhere on the UK, in this case from northern Britain and the Isle of Man, combined with experimental archaeology and contextual analysis, the author claims that battle-axeheads were essentially functional tools with a complex biography from source extraction (possibly from Scotland or the Lake District in the case of the Boltby example), through distribution, gift, exchange and use, to their final deposition (Roy 2020: 238). However, evidence of wood-chopping is not found on the finest examples (Sheridan pers. comm.). Manby too, on the basis of petrological evidence from the battle-axeheads and newly obtained isotopic evidence from the individuals interred with them, particularly for the Wolds (Montgomery *et al.* 2007; Jay *et al.* 2012: 231–4), asks whether battle-axeheads might not have been part of a package of grave goods brought in specially from elsewhere to accompany and confer status on the bodies, a question that can only be resolved through further petrological analysis of the battle-axeheads on the one hand and possibly isotope analysis of the skeletons on the other (Manby 2017: 122).

Excavation 2 (Dialstone Farm)

The second 'excavation' uncovered by Heys and Taylor in truth is perhaps better described as the discovery and collection of a number of significant items found only a week later at the beginning of March 1992 (Diary 3: 42–3). They were scattered across a small area on or close to the surface of the ploughsoil in one location which collectively pointed to a disturbed or destroyed Early Bronze Age grave somewhere in the vicinity. At a point in Hut Field, Dialstone Farm, to the south of the barrow at SE 5128 8429 (Figure 1.6: X), estimated at SE 5130 8408 (Figure 1.6: Y), they came across cremated bone fragments (Figs. 4.10–4.11), charcoal, characteristic Early Bronze Age sherds, some undecorated, others decorated with herringbone and others with fingernail-stabbed lines impressions and/or herringbone, two flint flakes and a small piece of broken chert. Being so close to the barrow, it is more than likely that the items, if not the flint and chert (which could well be casual losses), then at least the bone and broken pottery, came from there and were scattered by the plough. Interestingly, both barrows lie less than 50m to the west of a short stretch of Cleave Dyke, the system of boundaries constructed in the Late Bronze/Early Iron Age. At the time of writing (February 2023), the human remains await further analysis, i.e. radiocarbon dating, osteology, isotopic analysis, etc. Again, to quote the relevant entry in Taylor's diary:

'07.03.92 Sat. To Dialstone with Ronnie [work colleague] and Shirley [his wife]…To site found last week, take bearing and photo, layout 10' x 8' and commence to clear, odd sherds on top. Shirley tackled area of sherds – G.V. cleared to N and Ronnie to S. & E. Shirley soon down to black edge at base of ploughing – G.V. cleared towards reddened area. G.V. area dense reddened clay, intense discolouration but no sign of method of heating – 1" ploughed off and as layer in ploughing? Was it just basal clay as rest of site affected by heat? Shirley commenced clear-up of area, photo taken and measurements, broken pieces of stone around edges – very blackened underneath + bits of charcoal in whole mass. Odd potsherds and larger stone to one side but fairly central – other sherds, broken stones, charcoal and darkened soil in shallow hole (pit)? Sample placed in bucket including all broken stone pieces, sherds identified kept separate – Rusticated ware with fingernail stabs and lines (shallow groove) also 1 piece with herringbone pattern and grooved lines, other photo taken. G.V.T. hole very shallow, no sign of any extraneous material – back-filled on completion' (Diary 3, 42–3).

Figure 4.10: Cremated bone fragments (T4. B018.3) (20: Hut Field, Dialstone Farm)

0 1 2 3 4 5cm

Figure 4.11: Cremated bone fragments (T4.B018.4) (20: Hut Field, Dialstone Farm)

Excavation 3 (Murton Common)

The third excavation, in August 1995, was at the 'tumulus' marked on the OS map on Murton Common in the large field immediately north of the Boltby crossroads at SE 5102 8821 (Figure 1.6: C), from which it is believed a bronze spearhead had been recovered (Denny 1865: 499). Although ploughed down, the barrow was reported in 1951 as a 19m diameter circular mound and was still visible on the ground as a slight rise in 1976, which is probably how it appeared when Heys and Taylor trowelled into the mound in 1995. However, since 2009 it has disappeared from aerial view.

Working systematically across the surface of the mound by a series of parallel traverses (Figure 4.12), Heys and Taylor recovered a substantial quantity of large bone fragments including part of a lower jawbone complete with teeth still *in situ*, small cremated bone fragments, pieces of charcoal, a fragment of rock crystal and a few flint pieces (Figs. 4.13–4.16). The research potential here is clear: radiocarbon dating of the charcoal and the calcined bone, osteological assessment of the bone to establish gender, age and pathology, and isotope analysis of the teeth to investigate the individual's diet and origins. The following account is again taken directly from Taylor's diary:

'10.09.95 Sun. ...on to Murton long field at side of Drove road. Walked well worked and sown with crop. Started at gate by Silver Hills farm – proceeded slowly up field. Flint found on every pass – most unusual for the area. One huge core found (size of ½ brick). Also barrow mound spotted – not seen before although on NY Moors 1″ map – sited between White Barrow on edge of cliff near Upper Paradise's barrow behind Silver Hills farm on Murton estate – part of lower jaw with teeth and possible thigh bone from clump…

18.09.95 Mon. With David …To Murton large field alongside Drove road to continue walking parallel traverses. First look on barrow mound, further pieces of bone found – long bone and thick skull type bone, also possible hip joint socket and further small cremated pieces' (Diary 4, 95–6).'

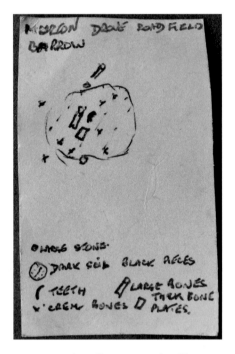

Figure 4.12: Plan of barrow mound and location of finds (with key) (Taylor) (41: Big Field, Murton SE 5102 8821) (faint broken parallel lines indicate the passes made over the mound by Heys and Taylor)

Figure 4.13: Large unburnt bone fragments (T4.B103.1–6) (41: Big Field, Murton SE 5102 8821)

Figure 4.14: Cremated bone fragments (T4.B103.7–41) (41: Big Field, Murton SE 5102 8821)

Figure 4.15: (Left) Lower jawbone fragment with teeth in situ (T4.B103.42) (41: Big Field, Murton SE 5102 8821)
Figure 4.16: (Right)Assorted pieces (T4.B103.43–48) (41: Big Field, Murton SE 5102 8821) 43: lump of charcoal, 44:
piece of quartz, 45–48: worked flakes

Central Region (Mesolithic Excavations)

'Pointed Stone' and Money Howe

In marked contrast to the south and west region components of the collection, which are almost entirely Neolithic and Bronze Age, with a scattering of Late Iron Age/Romano-British material, the material from the higher plateau of the ridges and dales to the north is dominated by the Early Mesolithic, gathered from some two dozen sites across the region, and in particular by material from two sets of specific excavations carried out on Bilsdale East Moor by the Taylors (i.e. Geoffrey and his wife, Shirley) in the 1970s: around the remains of the Early Bronze Age ring cairn at Money Howe (SE 593 951 approx.) (Location 170) (Figure 4.17) and at a cluster of sites known from their proximity to a conspicuous solitary pointed rock as 'Pointed Stone', further east on Bransdale Ridge (Location 177) (Figs. 4.18 and 4.19).

Though details of exactly where they dug were initially hard to establish, Jacobi describes how two of the three sites were excavated, 'Pointed Stone 2' and 'Pointed Stone 3', barely 20m apart, 'close to one of the highest points of the hills, at 410 metres O.D. on the eastern flank of Bilsdale East Moor, above Bransdale' (Jacobi 1978: 309). An annotated map drawn up by Taylor of the entire North York Moors central collecting area indicates the location for 'Pointed Stone' at a point directly south of the summit of the unnamed hill to the north of the head of Bonfield Gill at approximately SE 605 975, which agrees well with a sketch map of an assortment of sites at 'Pointed Stone', including both the systematically excavated areas as well as the sites for surface collection of flints, drawn up by Taylor at the time (Figure 4.20). This is confirmed by Spratt, who gives a broadly similar reference of SE 604 975 (Spratt 1993: table 4, 64 and table 5, 66). Eventually however, the precise locations of two of the three trenches, namely Pointed Stones I and II, were established by the North East Yorkshire Mesolithic Project at SE 6047 9746 and SE 6054 9744 (Waughman 2015: 18–19). According to Jacobi, two of the three excavations, a pair within 25m of each other at Pointed Stone, were carried out in 1974 and 1975 (Jacobi 1978: 309). Given that Taylor at that time was a working man, with only weekends and holidays off, this means that the two dates entered on his excavation plan of the site of 'June 23' and 'June 30' can only therefore refer to June 1974 (Figure 4.20). The site at Money Howe, SE 5937 9513, was given by Jacobi as '340m OD at the south-western end of Bilsdale Moor south-south-west of Pointed Stone' (Jacobi 1978: 321) and was excavated in 1975.

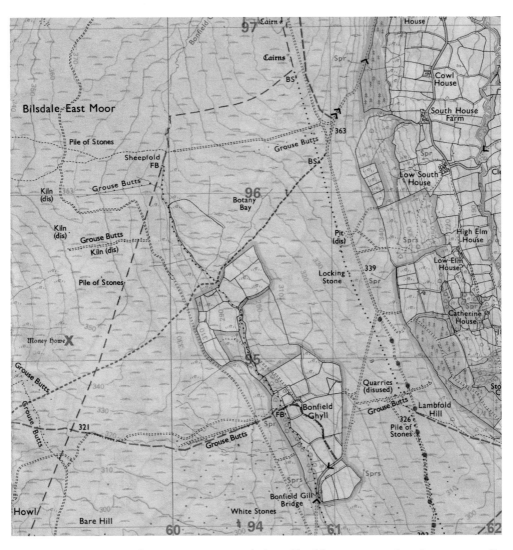

Figure 4.17: Estimated site of Money Howe excavation (indicated by x) (© Crown Copyright Ordnance Survey. All rights reserved)

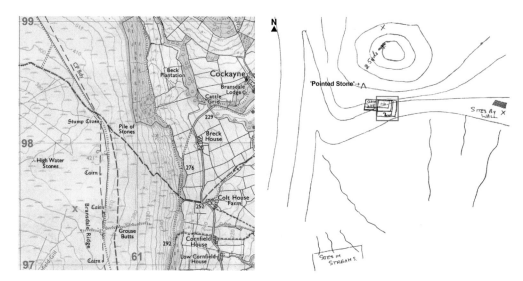

Figure 4.18: Estimated site of 'Pointed Stone' excavations area (indicated by x) (© Crown Copyright Ordnance Survey. All rights reserved)

Figure 4.19: Sketch map of sites at 'Pointed Stone', Bilsdale E Moor (Taylor) (Black square indicates excavation area illustrated in Figure 4.20)

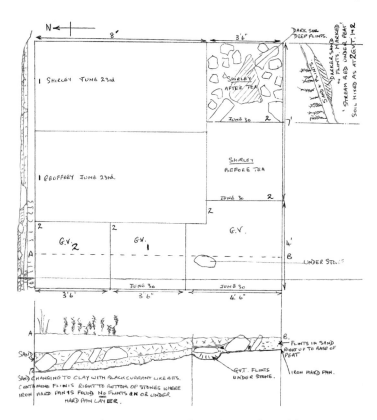

Figure 4.20: 'Pointed Stone' excavation plan and section (Taylor) (Area indicated by black square in Figure 4.19)

Jacobi reported a total of around 6500 worked flints at Pointed Stone: 2000 at 'Site 2' over an area of around 28m² and 4500 over 39m² at 'Site 3', up to 70% of which were microliths (Jacobi 1978: 311, 315). The bulk of the flints at 'Site 3' were found in three distinct clusters, many with signs of burning, along with substantial amounts of charcoal, and appeared to surround a relatively quiet central area, which Jacobi believed was a possible hearth. However, there was no evidence of any other 'structures'.

At Money Howe a roughly circular area 'some 7m across' was completely excavated, according to Jacobi revealing only a broad scatter of flints. Two areas were excavated labelled 'W' and 'N', but it is not clear from such records as exist in the Taylor collection whether it was a single site excavated in two parts, or two separate but immediately adjacent or nearby sites within the area. However, detailed grid maps of the excavated areas indicating the precise size as well as the nature and total number of lithic pieces were discovered within the collection by the author, and these reveal both the density and extent of the Early Mesolithic activity on the site, as well as the distribution of charcoal. Although plenty of charcoal was recovered within the Mesolithic layer (which could possibly be useful for dating purposes in terms of the species represented if it has not been contaminated), this was found to be broadly scattered across the entire site, with no particular concentration indicating a possible hearth or campfire area. Just under 5000 pieces were recovered from an area of 11yd x 20yd (10m x 18m) at Money Howe W and around 2000 pieces from two adjacent areas of 10yd x 10yd (9.1m x 9.1m) and 5yd x 5yd (4.6m x 4.6m) at Money Howe N. Taylor's grid maps of the excavations are not only a record of what was found but also illustrate the excavation technique which was used, first stripping the cover from the moorland surface to reveal the uppermost material, and then carefully trowelling the area in 1yd x 1yd grids, each identified by numbers running W–E and by letters N– S, and further divided into four quarters numbered 1–4. A full breakdown of the entire contents of each such square, including both worked pieces and waste, is available in the archive.

What is not clear is how much of the material remained in the possession of Jacobi, either retained by him to begin with or, as surviving correspondence between them indicates, sent to him by the Taylors for assessment, though it does not seem to have been that much. However, a summary of at least some of the material from both 'Pointed Stone' and Money Howe is given on the Jacobi database, Palaeolithic and Mesolithic Lithic Artefact (PaMeLA), by the Archaeology Database Service (ADS) (https://archaeologydataservice.ac.uk/archives/view/pamela_2014/results.cfm – enter Pointed Stone and Money Howe as search terms). The material at both sites consists essentially of cores and various forms of microliths and blades which Jacobi confidently attributed to the Early Mesolithic, quoting a radiocarbon date from unidentified charcoal fragments for the Money Howe Site 1 of 9430±390 BP (Q-1560: 9990–7609 cal BC) in the later Boreal when the climate was generally cool and dry and the upland would have had a covering of elm, hazel, oak and pine (Jacobi 1978: 297, 301, 308; Switsur and Jacobi 1979; Conneller *et al.* 2016: table 1). By today's considerably improved techniques of radiocarbon dating – and indeed by Jacobi's own admission at the time (1978: 297) – the excessively large standard deviation renders the date of questionable use. The material from Money Howe is described by Jacobi as of the 'Deepcar' type, named after the type-site in the Yorkshire Pennines (Radley and Mellars 1964), characterised by distinctly elongated, narrow, obliquely blunted points, frequent retouch along the leading edge, and points with convex blunting down the whole of one side, while the material from 'Pointed Stone' is of the 'Star

Carr' type – shorter, more angular obliquely blunted points, usually retouched down the leading edge, accompanied by isosceles triangles and trapezes (Jacobi 1978: 308–9; cf. Milner *et al.* 2018).

Based on this and on an analysis of the tool assemblage – low in scrapers but high in the production and repair of other tools (especially blades) – Jacobi interpreted the sites at 'Pointed Stone' and Money Howe as Early Mesolithic seasonal hunting camps, significantly situated in what would have been the ecozone between wooded and more open ground where the greatest number of animals would be found, serving the Early Mesolithic community based off the plateau at Star Carr on the shoreline of palaeo-Lake Flixton just over 40km to the ESE.

However, perhaps not that surprisingly, careful and comprehensive examination of this material (both worked and waste) by the author shows that, while mostly correct, Taylor's own identification of pieces, as opposed to Jacobi's, is not always completely reliable. But given the difficulty of confirming the precise identity of Mesolithic pieces, it still serves as a general guide to their sheer number, age and identity. It is as well before ending this section of the paper dealing with the Mesolithic, to quote Jacobi's acknowledgement to the Taylors:

> 'the discovery of the Maglemosian [i.e. what would now be termed Early Mesolithic] sites on the NYM is entirely the result of individual survey – in this case that of Mr and Mrs G.V. Taylor. Their work underlies the degree to which pre-Neolithic studies in the British Isles can still rely on private initiative to undertake critical fieldwork, often in hugely unattractive environments.' (Jacobi 1978: 327).

Nidderdale

South Haw, Masham Moor and Round Hill, Blubberhouses Moor

Before leaving this discussion of the Mesolithic material in the collection, there is however one further site worth mentioning. Though not on the North York Moors, it is one of the recognised sites in the Pennines: namely, the hill site of Little (or South) Haw on Masham Moor in Colsterdale, at 499m OD (Location 211, NGR SE 0870 7885) (Figure 4.21). Not to be confused with Great Haw (NGR 0752 7936), the summit of the hill at 542m OD, itself also a recognised Mesolithic site, or with another Little Haw, the summit of a second hill further north at 516m OD (NGR 0781 8030), South Haw is strangely missing off the definitive list of UK Mesolithic sites compiled by Wymer and Bonsall (Wymer and Bonsall 1977), presumably because it was unknown to them. To add to the confusion, Heys also gave the name 'Middle Haw' to an area where he found substantial amounts of Mesolithic material, lying roughly halfway between Great Haw and South Haw at SE 081 791.

As a substantial Mesolithic site, South Haw was believed to have been first discovered by Margaret Collins in 1976 (Moorhouse 1978b; Pastscape: MNY 24085; Chatterton 2005). She was the daughter of Ernest Rokeby Collins, an Army Major, First World War veteran and recipient of the D.S.O., who pioneered research into the early prehistory of this part of Yorkshire, including the Mesolithic (Collins 1930; 1933) and became a well-known figure in the area, serving as Chairman of the Prehistory Research Section of the Yorkshire Archaeological

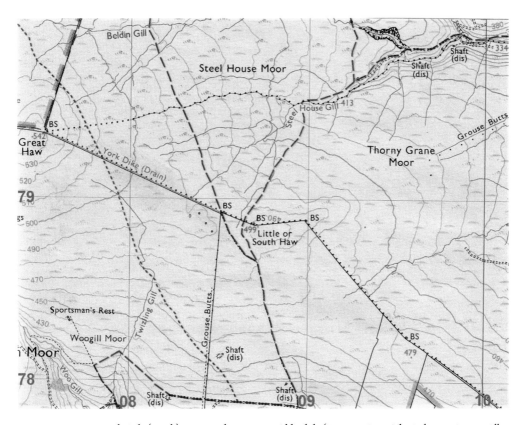

Figure 4.21: Great and Little (South) Haw, Masham Moor, Nidderdale (© Crown Copyright Ordnance Survey. All rights reserved)

Society from 1946–1962. However, Heys was apparently aware of the site from as early as 1962 (Chatterton 2005: 253) and what surviving material there is in his collection dates from the end of 1968. Margaret Collins continued to work on the site right up until shortly before her death in 2000 (Chatterton 2007). Large amounts of Late Mesolithic material (over 15,000), last known to be at Harrogate Museum, were recovered from an extensive area spread over most of the south-west approaches to its gentle summit. The site was further excavated and assessed by Richard Chatterton, a PhD student at the University of Manchester, between 2001 and 2005 (Chatterton 2005; 2008). Heys paid numerous visits to the area, accompanied on one occasion in 1991 by Taylor, when they carried out both surface collection and systematic trowelling of carefully selected areas, based on the evidence of surface finds. And again, as at 'Pointed Stone' and Money Howe, it was Jacobi who assessed Taylor's excavated material, which included cores, blades and microliths, surviving pieces of which, along with Heys' material, are depicted here for the first time (Figs. 4.22–4.27).

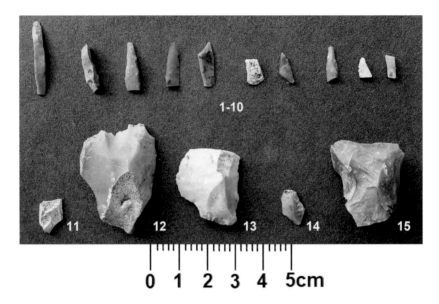

Figure 4.22: South Haw, Masham Moor SE 087 788 approx. (T18.1.1–15) 1–10: microliths, 11: retouched piece, 12–13: splinted pieces, 14: microlith by-product, 15: core

Figure 4.23: South Haw, Masham Moor SE 087 788 approx. (T18.1.16–21) 16: waste/pointed blade?, 17: blade (proximal fragment), 18: awl; 19–20: pointed blades. 21: notched pointed blade/burin

Figure 4.24: South Haw, Masham Moor SE 087 788 approx. (T18.1.22–29) 22–23: microliths, 24–25: retouched pieces, 26: splinted piece, 27–29: cores

Figure 4.25: South Haw, Masham Moor (T18.1.30–33) 30, 32–33: blades, 31: awl/borer

Figure 4.26: South Haw, Masham Moor SE 087 788 approx. (T18.1.34–38) 34–35: microliths, 36–37: cores, 38: chert core

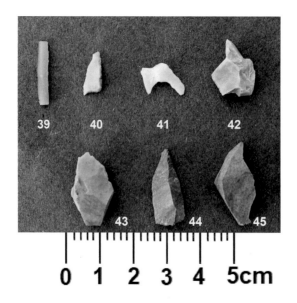

Figure 4.27: South Haw, Masham Moor SE 087 788 approx. (T18.1.39–45) 39: rod microlith, 40: microlith, 41: waste/ arrowhead (proximal fragment (?), 42: burin/borer (?), 43: worked flake, 44–45: chert waste/awls/borers (?)

There is not the space here nor would it be appropriate to go into all the Mesolithic material collected from all twenty-four sites (and very possibly more) identified by the Taylors, but the figures below, from Money Howe itself and elsewhere on Bilsdale Moor (Figs. 4.28–4.32), serve to give an illustration of just how abundant the material was. The identifications of the pieces from Round Hill, Blubberhouses Moor, in mid-Wharfedale, are also thanks to Jacobi (Figure 4.33).

Figure 4.28: 165: Arnsgill Ridge SE 524 967 (T5.237.1–15) 1–3: cores, 4: chert burin/blade, 5: retouched blade, 6: retouched blade (terminal fragment), 7–9: retouched blades, 10–15: microliths/microlith fragments

Figure 4.29: 171: Bilsdale West Moor, Cow Ridge, near Parci Gill ruins
SE 538 952 (T6.258.1–8) 1–4: retouched blades, 5-8: burins

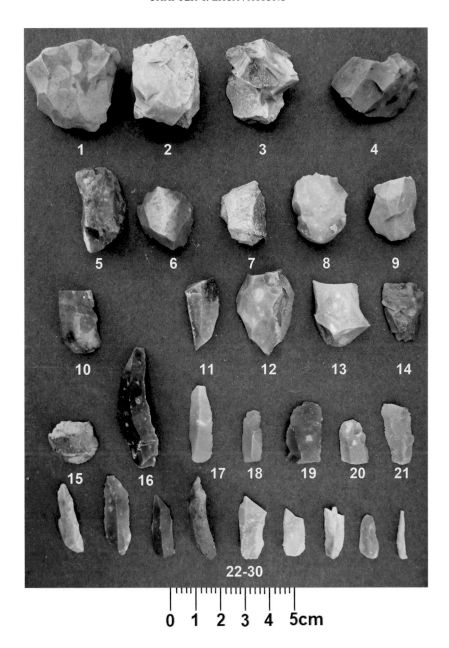

Figure 4.30: 171: Bilsdale West Moor (T7.300.1-30) 1-4,6,10,11: cores, 5,7-9: cores/waste, 12-14: waste, 15: thumb scraper, 16: retouched blade/plano-convex knife, 17-18: blades, 19-20: blades (terminal fragments), 21: blade (medial fragment), 22: notched pointed blade, 23-27: pointed blades, 28: retouched blade/awl, 29: microlithic blade (terminal fragment), 30: rod microlith

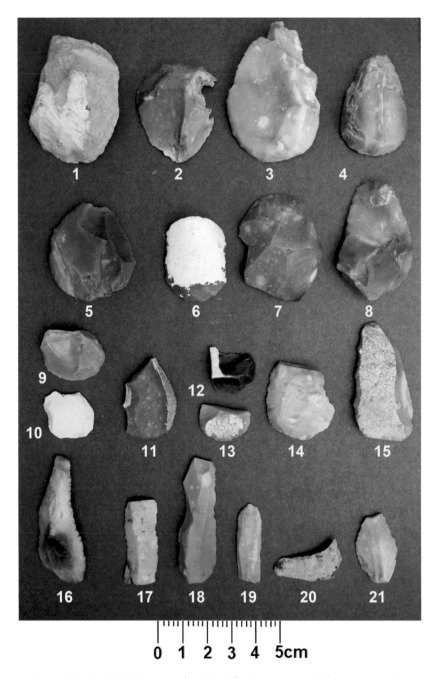

Figure 4.31: 181: Bilsdale East Moor (T8.352.1–21) 1–8: scrapers, 9–10: thumb scrapers, 11: scraper fragment, 12–13: thumb scraper fragments, 14: scraper, 15: worked flake, 16: saw, 17: denticulate blade/knife (medial fragment), 18: worked blade, 19: retouched flake/pointed blade?, 20: worked flake/right-angled awl?, 21: worked flake

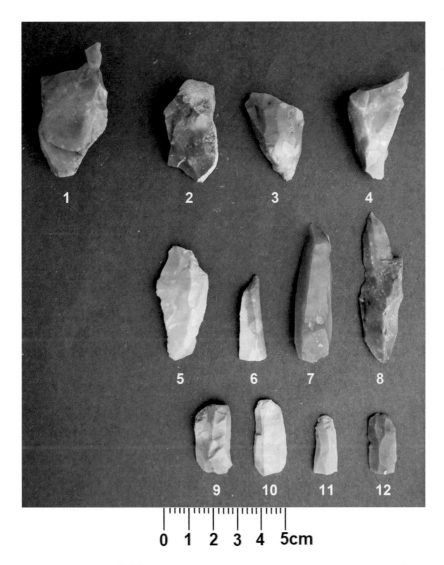

Figure 4.32: 179: Bilsdale East Moor: Money Howe SE 596 951 non-excavation material (T8.382.1–12) 1,2,4: waste, 3: core/waste, 5: retouched blade (fragment), 6,8: burins, 7: pointed blade, 9–10: blades, 11–12: blades (terminal fragments)

Figure 4.33: Round Hill N, Blubberhouses Moor SE 123 535 approx.
(T18.61.1–20) 1–3: waste/burins?, 4: blade, 5–6: burin spalls, 7:
microlith (retouched piece), 8–11: microliths (backed bladelets),
12–20: microliths (backed pieces)

Summary

Given the sheer combined size, diversity and range of the two collections, this book can do little more than provide a glimpse of them and has necessarily concentrated on just the material collected within the boundaries of Yorkshire. Nevertheless, the combined Taylor-Heys archive offers considerable potential for further serious research into the prehistoric period of the north of England, not only in Yorkshire but in regions outside Yorkshire too (particularly the Southern Pennines and Lincolnshire), making use of techniques such as radiocarbon dating, osteological examination, isotope analysis and X-ray fluorescence spectrometry, either unavailable or beyond the purse of the original collectors.

The sheer statistics of the combined collections speak for themselves. Discounting obvious waste and pieces too fragmentary to recognise, there are 19,540 worked items (Heys 2499;

Taylor 17,041), collected from 354 different sites, 224 (63%) of which were confined to the North York Moors (160 in the south and west region, 64 in the central region). These are backed up by the paper record contained in the Taylor diaries, describing no fewer than 745 visits amounting almost to obsession, mostly at weekends and during holiday periods, including four New Year's Eves (1987, 1989, 1991 and 1995), three New Year's Days (1984, 1987 and 1989), and one Boxing Day (1986), made between the beginning of December 1983 and Taylor's poignant last entry on 14th June 1997, when he was already terminally ill. At an average of 3–4 hours per visit, not counting travelling time to and from their respective homes in Oldham and Bradford, this amounts to well over a staggering 5000 man-hours of work, not to mention the mileage, carried out in all weathers. But it is to be remembered that they worked separately too: Taylor on collecting and on excavations of the higher central North York Moors with Jacobi in the 1970s, before the diaries begin, and Heys both before he met Taylor as early as 1961 and after Taylor's death until as recently as 2015. The Taylor-Heys archive, amassed over a lifetime of collecting, stands as a fine legacy to them both, and well deserves their place at last in the archaeological record.

Appendices

Appendix 1: Databases

Heys Database

http://doi.org/10.32028/9781803276427-Appendix-1a

Taylor Database

http://doi.org/10.32028/9781803276427-Appendix-1b

Appendix 2: Database of jet and jet-like items

http://doi.org/10.32028/9781803276427-Appendix-2

Heys Collection

Taylor Collection

Appendix 3: Locations of Sites

http://doi.org/10.32028/9781803276427-Appendix-3

Appendix 4: Figures & Photographs

http://doi.org/10.32028/9781803276427-Appendix-4

Heys Photographs

Taylor Figures

Sheets

Taylor Photographs

Sets

Databases 1-11, 15-16, 18, 21

Appendix 5: Taylor Diaries 1–4 (1983–1997)

http://doi.org/10.32028/9781803276427-Appendix-5

Appendix 6: Battle-axeheads from Yorkshire

http://doi.org/10.32028/9781803276427-Appendix-6

Appendix 7: Lincolnshire

http://doi.org/10.32028/9781803276427-Appendix-7

Appendix 1a

Heys Database

Appendix 1b

Taylor Database

Appendix 2

Database of jet and jet-like items

Appendix 3

Locations of Sites

Appendix 4

Figures & Photographs

Appendix 5

Taylor Diaries 1–4 (1983–1997)

Appendix 6

Battle-axeheads from Yorkshire

Appendix 7

Lincolnshire

Bibliography

Allason-Jones, L. 1996. *Roman Jet in the Yorkshire Museum*. York: The Yorkshire Museum.

Allason-Jones, L. (ed.) 2011. *Artefacts in Roman Britain: Their Purpose and Use*. Cambridge: Cambridge University Press.

Anderson, J., 1892. The nature of the discovery of a hoard of the Bronze Age consisting chiefly of personal ornaments of bronze, amber and gold at Balmashanner, near Forfar. *Proceedings of the Society of Antiquaries of Scotland* 26 (1891–2): 182–8.

Ashbee, P. 1960. *The Bronze Age Round Barrow in Britain: An Introduction to the Study of the Funerary Practice and Culture of the British and Irish Single-Grave People of the Second Millennium B.C.* London: Phoenix House.

Atkinson, J.C. 1863. Further Researches in Cleveland Grave-Hills. *Gentleman's Magazine* 15 (November): 548–52.

Atkinson, J.C. 1864. Excavation of a Large Howe on Skelton Moors in Cleveland. *Gentleman's Magazine* 16 (June): 705–9.

Ballin, T.B. 2008. The distribution of Arran pitchstone: territories, exchange and the 'English problem'. *PAST: The Newsletter of the Prehistoric Society* 60: 10–13.

Ballin, T.B. 2009. *Archaeological pitchstone in northern Britain: characterization and interpretation of an important prehistoric source*. BAR British Series 476. Oxford: BAR Publishing.

Ballin, T.B. 2011. *Overhowden and Airhouse, Scottish Borders: characterization and interpretation of two spectacular lithic assemblages from sites near the Overhowden henge*. BAR British Series 539. Oxford: BAR Publishing.

Ballin, T.B. 2015a. Arran pitchstone (Scottish volcanic glass): New dating evidence. *Journal of Lithic Studies* 2 (No. 1): 5–16.

Ballin, T.B. 2015b. Arran pitchstone ('Scottish obsidian') – new dating evidence. *PAST: The Newsletter of the Prehistoric Society* 79 (April): 1–3.

Bateman, T. 1861. *Ten Years' Diggings in Celtic and Saxon Grave Hills, in the Counties of Derby, Stafford and York*. London: J.R. Smith; Derby: Bemrose.

Boughey, K. 2010. Mitchell Laithes Revisited. *Prehistory Research Section Bulletin of the Yorkshire Archaeological Society* 47: 2.

Boughey, K. 2015. *Life and Death in Prehistoric Craven: Welbury Wilkinson Holgate and the Excavation of the Hare Hill Ring Cairn*. Leeds: Yorkshire Archaeological Society.

Boughey, K. 2018. Dates from Collared Urn Burials in Yorkshire (recent work). *Prehistoric Yorkshire* 55: 71–2.

Boughey, K. 2019. Boltby Urns: An Overview of the Evidence. *Prehistoric Yorkshire* 56: 66–83.

Boughey, K. 2020. Pots of Confusion: Bronze Age Vessels from Baildon. *Prehistoric Yorkshire* 57: 84–117.

Bradley, P. with Edwards, G. 2011. The shale armlet from the Long Barrow. In Harding, J. and Healy, F. (eds), *The Raunds Area Project, Volume 2 – Supplementary studies*, 400. Swindon: English Heritage.

Brindley, A. 2007. *The Dating of Food Vessels and Urns in Ireland*. Galway: National University of Ireland, Galway.

Brück, J. and Davies, A. 2018. The social role of non-metal 'valuables' in Late Bronze Age Britain. *Cambridge Archaeological Journal* 28(4): 665–88. Viewed 2 September 2022, <https:// doi.org/ 10.1017/ S095977431800029X> .

Burgess, A. 2001. Manor Farm. In Roberts *et al.*, 72–82.

Burgess, C.B. 1986. "Urnes of no small variety". Collared Urns reviewed. *Proceedings of the Prehistoric Society* 52: 339–51.

Calder, C.S.T. 1950. Report on a Bronze Age grave discovered on Cumledge Estate near Duns. *History of the Berwickshire Naturalists' Club* 32(1): 46–8.

Callander, J.G. 1916. Notice of a jet necklace found in a cist in a Bronze Age cemetery, discovered on Burgie Lodge Farm, Morayshire, with notes on Scottish prehistoric jet ornaments. *Proceedings of the Society of Antiquaries of Scotland* 50 (1915–16): 201–40.

Card, N., Edmonds, M. and Mitchell, A. 2020. *The Ness of Brodgar: As it Stands.* Kirkwall: Kirkwall Press.

Challis, A.J. and Harding, D.W. 1975. *Later Prehistory from the Trent to the Tyne.* BAR British Series 20. Oxford: BAR Publishing.

Chatterton, R. 2005. Transition and persistence: material culture in the Mesolithic landscape of North Yorkshire. Unpublished PhD dissertation. University of Manchester. Viewed 4 November 2020, <http://ethos.bl.uk/OrderDetails.Do?uin=uk.bl.ethos.535553>.

Chatterton, R. 2007. South Haw: An Upland Mesolithic Site in its Local and Regional Context. In Waddington, C. and Pedersen, K. (eds), *Mesolithic Studies In The North Sea Basin And Beyond*, Chapter 10. Oxford: Oxbow.

Chowne, P. forthcoming. *Prehistoric Lincolnshire.* Lincoln: Lincolnshire Local History Society.

Clark, J.G.D. 1929. Discoidal polished flint knives – their typology and distribution. *Proceedings of the Prehistoric Society of East Anglia* 6: 41–5.

Clarke, D.L. 1970. *Beaker Pottery of Great Britain and Ireland.* Cambridge: Cambridge University Press.

Clarke, D.V., Cowie, T.G. and Foxon, A. 1985. *Symbols of Power at the Time of Stonehenge.* Edinburgh: Her Majesty's Stationery Office.

Clough, T.H.McK. and Cummins, W.A. 1988. (eds). *Stone Axe Studies. Vol.2.* CBA Research Report No. 67.

Collins, E.R. 1930. The Palaeolithic Implements of Nidderdale, Yorkshire. *Proceedings of the Prehistoric Society of East Anglia* 6(3): 156–71.

Collins, E.R. 1933. Upper Palaeolithic Sites in Nidderdale. *Proceedings of the Prehistoric Society of East Anglia* 7(2): 185–7.

Conneller, C., Bayliss, A., Milner, N. and Taylor, B. 2016. The Resettlement of the British Landscape: Towards a chronology of Early Mesolithic lithic assemblage types. *Internet Archaeology* 42: 1–2. Viewed 1 September 2022, <https://doi.org/10.11141/ia.42.11 and https://core.ac.uk/download/pdf/157853571.pdf>.

Cowling, E.T. 1948. *Rombalds Way. A Prehistory of Mid-Wharfedale.* Otley: William Walker and Sons Ltd.

Cowling, E.T. 1963. Two Discoidal Flint Knives from Yorkshire. *Yorkshire Archaeological Journal* 41: 17–18.

Denford, G.T. 2000. *Prehistoric and Romano-British Kimmeridge Shale.* Winchester: Winchester Museums Service. Viewed 2 September 2022, <https://doi.org/10.5284/1000090>.

Denny, H. 1859. Notice of early British tumuli on the Hambleton Hills, near Thirsk. *Proceedings of the Yorkshire Geological and Polytechnic Society* 4: 488–502.

Dent, J.S. 1983. Summary of the Excavations carried out in Garton Slack and Wetwang Slack 1964–80. *East Riding Archaeologist* 7: 1–13.

Department of the Environment, Ancient Monuments and Historic Buildings. 1978. *List of ancient monuments in England: Volume 1 Northern England.* London: DOE.

Durden, T. 1995. The production of specialised flintwork in the later Neolithic: a case study from the Yorkshire Wolds. *Proceedings of the Prehistoric Society* 61: 409–32.

Elgee, F. 1930. *Early Man in North-East Yorkshire.* Gloucester: John Bellows.

Elgee, F. and Elgee, H.W. 1949. An Early Bronze Age burial in a boat-shaped wooden coffin, from north-east Yorkshire. *Proceedings of the Prehistoric Society* 15: 87–106.

Evans, J. 1872. *The Ancient Stone Implements, Weapons and Ornaments of Great Britain.* London: Longman, Green, Reader and Dyer.

Evans, J. 1897. 2nd edn. *The Ancient Stone Implements, Weapons and Ornaments of Great Britain.* London: Longmans, Green, and Co.

Everson, P. 1974. An excavated Anglo-Saxon sunken-featured building and settlement site at Salmonby, Lincs. 1972. *Lincolnshire History and Archaeology* 9: 61–72.

Fitzpatrick, A.W. 2011. *The Amesbury Archer and the Boscombe Bowmen. Bell Beaker burials on Boscombe Down, Amesbury, Wiltshire.* Salisbury: Wessex Archaeology Report 27.

Fokkens, H., Achterkamp, Y. and Kuijpers, M. 2008. Bracers or Bracelets? About the Functionality of Bell Beaker Wrist-guards. *Proceedings of the Prehistoric Society* 74: 107–40.

Fortey, N.J., Cooper, A.H., Henney, P.J., Colman, T. and Nancarrow, P.H.A. 1994. Appinitic intrusions in the English Lake District. *Mineralogy Report* 51: 355–75.

Gardiner, J. 2008. On the production of discoidal flint knives and changing patterns of specialist flint procurement in the Neolithic on the South Downs, England. In Fokkens, H., Coles, B.J., Van Gun, A.L., Kleijne, J.P., Ponje, H.H. and Appendel, C.G. (eds), *Between Foraging and Farming*, 235-46. Leiden: University of Leiden. Viewed 11 March 2022, <https://www.sidestone.com/books/ between-foraging-and-farming>.

Gaunt, G.D. and Buckland, P.C. 2003. The Geological Background to Yorkshire's Archaeology. In Manby *et al.*, 17–23.

Gibson, A.M., Bayliss, A., Heard, H., Mainland, I., Ogden, A.R., Bronk Ramsey, C., Cook, G., van der Plicht, J. and Marshall, P. 2009 Recent research at Duggleby Howe, North Yorkshire. *Archaeological Journal* 166(1): 39-78.

Gilks, J.A. 1981. A Beaker Battle-Axe from Thurstonland, near Huddersfield, and Its Relative Date. *Yorkshire Archaeological Journal* 53: 7–11.

Green, B. 1988. The petrological identification of stone implements from East Anglia. In Clough, T.H.McK. and Cummins, W.A. (eds), *Stone Axe Studies. Vol.2*, 36-407. CBA Research Report No. 6.

Green, H.S. 1980. *The Flint Arrowheads of the British Isles. A detailed study of material from England and Wales with comparanda from Scotland and Ireland.* BAR British Series 75. Oxford: BAR Publishing.

Greenwell, W. 1865. Notices of the examinations of ancient grave-hills in the North Riding of Yorkshire. *Archaeological Journal* 22: 97–117, 241–63.

Greenwell, W. and Rolleston, G. 1877. *British Barrows.* Oxford: Oxford University Press.

Harwood-Long, W. (ed.). 1963. Yorkshire Archaeological Register. Boltby. N.R. *Yorkshire Archaeological Journal* 41: 3.

Hayes, R.H. 1963a. Boltby. N.R. Yorkshire Archaeological Register. *Yorkshire Archaeological Journal* 41: 3.

Hayes, R.H. 1963b. Archaeology 2: The Early Bronze Age 1700-1400 BC and Middle Bronze Age 1400–700 BC. In McDonnell, J. (ed.), *A History of Helmsley, Rievaulx and District*, 31–53. York: Stonegate Press.

Hayes, R.H. 1964. Baysdale, N.R. *Yorkshire Archaeological Journal* 41: 163–4.

Hayes, R.H. 1978. Excavation of Barrows at Lingmoor, Hutton-le-Hole, North Yorkshire. *Yorkshire Archaeological Journal* 50: 31–4.

Healy, F., Marshall, P., Bayliss, A., Cook, G., Bronk Ramsey, C., van der Plicht, J. and Dunbar, E. 2018. When and why? The chronology and context of flint mining at Grime's Graves, Norfolk, England. *Proceedings of the Prehistoric Society* 84: 277–301.

Hearne, T. (ed.). 1769. *Leland's Itinerary* 3rd edn. Vol. IV. Oxford: T. Hearne

Henderson, J., Sheridan, J.A., Chenery, S., Evans, J., Timberlake, S., Towle, A., Knight, M., Wiseman, R. and Troalen, L. forthcoming. Beads. In Knight, M., Ballantyne, R., Brudenell, M., Cooper, A., Gibson D. and Robinson Zeki, I. (eds), *The Must Farm Pile-dwelling Settlement. Volume 2: Specialist Reports.* CAU Must Farm/Flag Fen Basin Depth & Time Series Volume II. Cambridge: McDonald Institute for Archaeological Research.

Heys, D.J. and Taylor, G.V. 1998. A Bronze Age Urn Burial from Boltby, North York Moors. *Prehistory Research Section Bulletin of the Yorkshire Archaeological Society* 35: 9–18.

History and Topography of the City of York: and the North Riding of Yorkshire. 1859. Beverley: T. Whellan and Co.

Howarth, E. 1899. *Catalogue of the Bateman Collection of Antiquities in the Sheffield Museum.* Sheffield: Free Public Libraries and Museum.

Viewed 26 March 2022, <https://archaeologydataservice.ac.uk/archives/view/pamela_2014/results. cfm>.

Viewed 8 March 2021, <https://en.m.wikipedia.org/wiki/Ness_of_Brodgar>.

Viewed 26 March 2022, https://www.british museum.org/collection /search?keyword=Boltby.

Viewed at various times between 23 November 2019 and 26 October 2020, <https://www. pastscape. org.uk>.

Viewed 7 March 2021, <https://www.turnstone.ca/appin.htm>.

Viewed 26 February 2021, <https://www.wessexarch.co.uk/our-work/amesbury-archer>.

Viewed 21 February 2021, <https://www.yorkmuseumstrust.org.uk/collections>.

Hunter, F.J. 1998. Cannel coal "napkin ring". In Strachan, R., Ralston, I.B.M. and Finlayson, B, Neolithic and later prehistoric structures, and early medieval metal-working at Blairhall Burn, Amisfield, Dumfriesshire, 79–82. *Proceedings of the Society of Antiquaries of Scotland* 128: 55–94.

Hunter, F.J. 2007. The cannel coal. In Ellis, C. Total excavation of a later prehistoric enclosure at Braehead, Glasgow, 204–19. *Proceedings of the Society of Antiquaries of Scotland* 137: 179–264.

Hunter, F.J. 2016. 'Coal money' from Portpatrick (south-west Scotland): reconstructing an Early Medieval craft centre from antiquarian finds. In Hunter, F.J. and Sheridan, J.A. (eds), *Ancient Lives: object, people and place in early Scotland. Essays for David V Clarke on his 70th birthday*, 281–302.

Hunter, F.J. 2021. Shale and cannel coal. In O'Connell, C. and Anderson, S., *Excavations in a prehistoric landscape at Blackford, Perth and Kinross, 2007–8*, 30. *Scottish Archaeological Internet Report* 93. Viewed 2 September 2022, <https://doi.org/10.9750/issn.2056-7421.2021.93>.

Hunter, F.J. and Ward, T. 2021. F24/188 & 189. Cannel coal 'napkin ring' fasteners. In Ward 2021, 69–71.

Ivleva, N. 2018. Romano-British glass bangles. *Roman Finds Group Datasheet* 9, 1–6. Viewed 2 September 2022, <https://scholarlypublications.universiteitleiden.nl/acess/item%3A297 2588/view>.

Ixer, R. and Davis, R.V. 1998. Petrology Report. In Heys, D.J. and Taylor, G.V. 1998. A Bronze Age Urn Burial from Boltby, North York Moors. *Prehistory Research Section Bulletin of the Yorkshire Archaeological Society* 35: 16.

Jacobi, R. 1978. Northern England in the eighth millennium bc: an essay. In Mellars, P.A. (ed.), *The Early Postglacial Settlement of Northern Europe*, 295–332. London: Duckworth.

Jay, M., Parker Pearson, M., Richards, M., Nehrlich, O., Montgomery, J., Chamberlain, A. and Sheridan, A. 2012. The Beaker People Project: an interim report on the progress of the isotopic analysis of the organic skeletal material. In Allen, M.J., Gardiner, J. and Sheridan, A. (eds), *Is There a British Chalcolithic: People, place and polity in the late 3rd millennium*, 226-36. Oxford: Prehistoric Society Research Paper 4.

Johnstone, G.S. and Mykura, W. 1989. *British Regional Geology: Northern Highlands of Scotland*. 4th edn. Nottingham: British Geological Survey.

Keen, L. and Radley, J. 1971. Report on petrological identification of stone axes from Yorkshire. *Proceedings of the Prehistoric Society* 27: 16–37.

Kemble, J.M. 1864. *Horae Ferales; or studies in the archaeology of the Northern Nations*. London: Lovell, Reeve & Co.

Kenworthy, J.B. 1977. A reconsideration of the 'Ardiffery' finds, Cruden, Aberdeenshire. *Proceedings of the Society of Antiquaries of Scotland* 108 (1976–7): 80–93.

Kilbride-Jones, H.E. 1938. Glass armlets in Britain. *Proceedings of the Society of Antiquaries of Scotland* 72: 366–95.

Kinnes, I.A. and Cook, J. 1998. The burials. In Kinnes, I.A., Cameron, F., Trow, S. and Thomson, D. *Excavations at Cliffe, Kent*, 59–62. British Museum Occasional Paper 69. London: The British Museum.

Kinnes, I.A. and Longworth, I.H. 1985. *Catalogue of the Excavated Prehistoric and Romano-British Material in the Greenwell Collection*. London: British Museum Publications Ltd.

Knox, R. 1855. *Descriptions geological, topographical and antiquarian in Eastern Yorkshire between the rivers Humber and Tees*. London: Robert Knox.

Longworth, I.H. 1984. *Collared Urns of the Bronze Age in Great Britain and Ireland*. Cambridge: Cambridge University Press.

Lynch, F. 1991. *Prehistoric Anglesey: the archaeology of the Island to the Roman Conquest*. Anglesey: Anglesey Antiquarian Society.

Mackay, W.A. 1979. A Discoidal Knife from Kepwick and Neolithic Finds From Pocklington. *Yorkshire Archaeological Journal* 51: 137–9.

Machin, M.L. and Beswick, P. 1975. Further excavations of the enclosure at Swine Sty, Big Moor, Baslow, and a report on the shale industry at Swine Sty. *Transactions of the Hunter Archaeological Society* 10: 204–11.

Manby, T.G. 1974. Grooved Ware sites in the north of England. BAR British Series 9. Oxford: BAR Publishing.

Manby, T.G. 1998a. Obituary. *Prehistory Research Section Bulletin of the Yorkshire Archaeological Society* 35: 7.

Manby, T.G. 1998b. The Pottery. In Heys, D.J. and Taylor, G.V. 1998. A Bronze Age Urn Burial from Boltby, North York Moors. *Prehistory Research Section Bulletin of the Yorkshire Archaeological Society* 35: 12–13.

Manby, T.G. 1998c. The Battle Axe. In Heys, D.J. and Taylor, G.V. 1998. A Bronze Age Urn Burial from Boltby, North York Moors. *Prehistory Research Section Bulletin of the Yorkshire Archaeological Society* 35: 15.

Manby, T.G. 2001. The Earlier Prehistoric Archaeology Of The Vale Of York. In Kershaw, A., Horne, P., MacLeod, D. and Oakey, M. (eds). 2020. *'A perfect flat'. Understanding the archaeology of the Vale of York*, 31–89. Historic England Research Report Series No. 272-2020 Viewed 15 March 2021, <https://historicengland.org.uk/research/results/reports/272-2020>.

Manby, T.G. 2003. The Late Upper Palaeolithic and Mesolithic Periods in Yorkshire. In Manby *et al.*, 31–33.

Manby, T.G. 2017. Stone Battle Axe Production In Yorkshire. In Shaffrey, R. (ed.), *Written In Stone: Papers on the function, form, and provenancing of prehistoric stone objects in memory of Fiona Roe*, 111–27. Oxford: Highfield Press.

Manby, T.G., King, A. and Vyner, B. 2003. The Neolithic and Bronze Ages: a Time of Early Agriculture. In Manby *et al.*, 35–113.

Manby, T.G., Moorhouse, S. and Ottaway, P. (eds). 2003. *The Archaeology of Yorkshire: an assessment at the beginning of the 21st century*. Yorkshire Archaeological Society Occasional Paper No. 3. Leeds: Yorkshire Archaeological Society.

May, J. 1977. *Prehistoric Lincolnshire*. Lincoln: Lincolnshire Local History Society.

Meegan, M. 2009. Shouldered Points from North-East Yorkshire and the Lower Wharfe. *Prehistory Research Section Bulletin* 46: 12–14.

Meegan, M. 2011. A Collection of Arrowheads from Hambeleton Down. *Prehistory Research Section Bulletin* 48: 42–5.

Metzger, M. 2018. Functional Analysis of Polished-Edge Discoidal Knives of the British Isles. *Lithics* 39: 77–9.

Milner, N., Conneller, C. and Taylor, B. 2018 (eds). *Star Carr Volume 1: A persistent place in a changing world. Volume 2: Studies in technology, subsistence and environment*. York: White Rose University Press. Viewed 19 November 2021, <https://universitypress.whiterose. ac.uk/site/books/ e/10.22599/book1 and <https://universitypress.whiterose.ac.uk/site/ books/e/10.22599/book2>.

Montgomery, J., Cooper, R.E. and Evans, J.A. 2007. Foragers, farmers or foreigners?: An assessment of dietary strontium isotope variation in the Middle Neolithic and Early Bronze Age East Yorkshire. In Larsson, M. and Parker Pearson, M. (eds), *From Stonehenge to the Baltic: Living with cultural diversity in the third millennium BC*, 65–75. BAR International Series 1629. Oxford: BAR Publishing.

Moorhouse, S. (ed.). 1978a. Yorkshire Archaeological Register for 1977. Hambleton Down. *Yorkshire Archaeological Journal* 50: 8.

Moorhouse, S. (ed.). 1978b. Yorkshire Archaeological Register for 1977. Stonebeck Up. *Yorkshire Archaeological Journal* 50: 9.

Mortimer, J.R. 1905. *Forty Years' Researches in British and Saxon Burial Mounds of East Yorkshire*. London and Hull: A. Brown & Sons Ltd.

Mytum, H. 1988. A battle-axe from Appleton Roebuck. *Yorkshire Archaeological Journal* 60: 175–6.

Neal, D.S. 1996. *Excavations on the Roman Villa at Beadlam, Yorkshire*. Yorkshire Archaeological Report 2.

Needham, A., Croft, S., Kröger, R., Robson, H.K., Rowley, C.C.A., Taylor, B., Gray Jones, A. and Conneller, C. 2018. The application of micro-Raman for the analysis of ochre artefacts from Mesolithic palaeo-lake Flixton. *Journal of Archaeological Science Reports* 17 (Feb. 2018): 650–6. Viewed 28 December 2020, <https://www.sciencedirect.com/science/article/ pii/S2352409X1730 5059>. And viewed 17 February 2018, <https://doi.org/10.1016/j. jasrep.2017.12.002>.

Needham, S.P. 2000. Metalwork. In Hughes, G. and Bevan, L., The Lockington Gold Hoard: an early Bronze Age barrow cemetery at Lockington, Leicestershire, 23–47. Oxford: Oxbow.

Needham, S.P. 2004. Migdale-Marnoch: sunburst of Scottish metallurgy. In Shepherd, I.A.G. and Barclay, G.J. (eds), *Scotland in Ancient Europe: the Neolithic and Early Bronze Age of Scotland in their European context*, 217–45. Edinburgh: Society of Antiquaries of Scotland.

Needham, S.P. 2005. Transforming Beaker culture in north-west Europe; processes of fusion and fission. *Proceedings of the Prehistoric Society* 71: 171–217.

Needham, S.P. 2015. Items of Equipment I: Daggers, Pommels and Belt Fittings. In Woodward and Hunter, 23–68.

Needham, S.P., Lawson, A. and Woodward, A. 2010. "A noble group of barrows": Bush Barrow and the Normanton Down Early Bronze Age cemetery two centuries on. *Antiquaries Journal* 90: 1–39.

Ordnance Survey Map Sheet 72. 1: 10560 (1 in.: mile). 1856.

Ordnance Survey Leisure Guide. North York Moors. (new edn.). 1992. London and Southampton: Automobile Association and Ordnance Survey.

OS Explorer OL26. North York Moors. Western Area. 2017. Southampton: Ordnance Survey.

OS Explorer OL27. North York Moors. Eastern Area. 2017. Southampton: Ordnance Survey.

Page, W. (ed.). 1907. *The Victoria County History of the County of York Vol. 1.* London: Eyre and Spottiswoode.

Paynter, S., Crew, P., Campbell, R., Hunter, F.J. and Jackson, C. 2022. Glass bangles in the British Isles: a study of trade, recycling and technology in the first and second centuries AD. *Antiquaries Journal,* 102: 15–44. Available online: https://10.1017/ S0003581521000378. [Accessed: 2/9/2022].

Phillips, P. 1997. Obituary. G.V. Taylor, 1924–1997. *Lincolnshire History & Archaeology* 32: 7.

Phillips, P., Cummins, W.A. and Keen, L. 1988. The petrological identification of stone implements from Yorkshire: second report. In Clough, T.H.McK. and Cummins, W.A. (eds), *Stone Axe Studies. Vol. 2,* 52–9. CBA Research Report No. 67.

Phillips, P., Field, F.N. and Taylor, G.V. 1990. Bronze Age Cemeteries and Flint Industries from Salmonby. *Lincolnshire History and Archaeology* 25: 5–11.

Pierpoint, S. and Phillips, P. 1978. A Grave-Group from Levisham Moor, North Yorkshire. *Yorkshire Archaeological Journal* 50: 43–8.

Price, J. 1988. Romano-British glass bangles from East Yorkshire. In Price, J. and Wilson, P.R. (eds), *Recent Research in Roman Yorkshire,* 339–66. BAR British Series 193. Oxford: BAR Publishing.

Radley, J. 1974. The Prehistory of the Vale of York. *Yorkshire Archaeological Journal* 46: 10–22.

Radley, J. and Mellars, P.A. 1964. A Mesolithic structure at Deepcar, Yorkshire, England, and the affinities of its associated flint industries. *Proceedings of the Prehistoric Society* 7: 1–24.

Richardson, J. and Vyner, B. 2010. Stanbury 'battle axe' burial – update. *Prehistory Research Section Bulletin of the Yorkshire Archaeological Society* 47: 50.

Richardson, J. and Vyner, B. 2011 An Exotic Early Bronze Age Funerary Assemblage from Stanbury, West Yorkshire. *Proceedings of the Prehistoric Society* 77: 49–63.

Roberts, I., Burgess, A. and Berg, D. (eds). 2001. *A New Link to the Past: the Archaeological Landscape of the M1-A1 Link Road. Yorkshire Archaeology No. 7.* Leeds: West Yorkshire Archaeology Service.

Roberts, I. and Weston, P. 2016. Excavations at Rossington Grange Farm. *Yorkshire Archaeological Journal* 88: 1–37.

Roe, F.E.S. 1966. The Battle-Axe Series in Great Britain. *Proceedings of the Prehistoric Society* 32: 199–245.

Roe, F.E.S. 1979. Typology of stone implements with shaft-holes. In Clough, T.H.McK. and Cummins, W.A. (eds), *Stone Axe Studies Vol. 1.* CBA Research Report No. 23, 23–48.

Roe, F. and Radley, J. 1968. Pebble Mace Heads With Hour-Glass Perforations from Yorkshire, Nottinghamshire and Derbyshire. *Yorkshire Archaeological Journal* 42: 169–77.

Roy, A.S. 2020. The Use and Significance of Early Bronze Age Stone Battle-axes and Axe-hammers from Northern Britain and the Isle of Man. *Proceedings of the Prehistoric Society* 86: 237–60, Viewed 24 January 2021, <https://www.cambridge.org/core/journals/proceedings-of-the- prehistoric-society/volume/AD9C16E0 FBAD05D22F4E44F37D43ED8A>.

Shepherd, I.A.G. 2009. The V-bored buttons of Great Britain and Ireland. *Proceedings of the Prehistoric Society* 75: 335–69.

Sheridan, J.A. 2004. The National Museums' of Scotland radiocarbon dating programmes: results obtained during 2003/4. *Discovery and Excavation in Scotland* 5: 174–6.

Sheridan, J.A. 2007a. Dating the Scottish Bronze Age: "There is clearly much that the material can still tell us", in Burgess, C,Topping, P. and Lynch, F. (eds), *Beyond Stonehenge: Essays on the Bronze Age in Honour of Colin Burgess*, 162–85. Oxford: Oxbow.

Sheridan, J.A. 2007b. The large elliptical Neolithic bead fragment, in M. Cook, Early Neolithic ritual activity, Bronze Age occupation and medieval activity at Pitlethie Road, Leuchars, Fife, 14–16. *Tayside and Fife Archaeological Journal* 13: 1–23.

Sheridan, J.A. 2007c. The bone belt hook from Bargrennan Pit 2, in V. Cummings and C. Fowler (eds), *From Cairn to Cemetery: an archaeological investigation of the chambered cairns and Early Bronze Age mortuary deposits at Cairnderry and Bargrennan White Cairn, south-west Scotland*, 112–124. Oxford: British Archaeological Reports (British Series 434).

Sheridan, J.A. 2012. The jet belt slider, Movers Lane. In Stafford, E., Goodburn, D. and Bates, M., *Landscape and Prehistory of the East London Wetlands. Investigations Along the A13 DBFO Roadscheme, Tower Hamlets, Newham and Barking and Dagenham, 2000-2003*, 192–202. Oxford: Oxford Archaeology (Monograph 17).

Sheridan, J.A. 2015a. V-Perforated Buttons. In Woodward and Hunter, 148–71.

Sheridan, J.A. 2015b. Discussion of disc bead and spacer plate necklaces of jet and jet-like materials. In Woodward and Hunter, 341–362.

Sheridan, J.A. and Davis, M. 1998. The Welsh 'jet set' in prehistory: a case of keeping up with the Joneses? In Gibson, A.M. and Simpson, D.D.A. (eds), *Prehistoric Ritual and Religion*, 148–62. Stroud: Sutton.

Sheridan, J.A. and Davis, M. 2002. Investigating jet and jet-like artefacts from prehistoric Scotland: the National Museums of Scotland project. *Antiquity* 76: 812–25.

Sheridan, J.A., Brunning, R., Straker, V., Campbell, G., Cartwright, C., King, S. and Quinnell, H. 2016. The wooden studs. In Jones, A.M., *Preserved in the Peat. An Extraordinary Bronze Age Burial on Whitehorse Hill, Dartmoor, and its Wider Context*, 117–145. Oxford: Oxbow.

Smith, J. 2006. Early Bronze Age Stone Wrist-Guards in Britain: archer's bracer or social symbol? Viewed 22 October 2020, http://www.geocities.com/archchaos1/article1/1.htm>.

Smith, M. 1978. A Beaker burial from Hambleton Moor. *Ryedale Historian* 9: 22–8.

Smith, M.J.B. 1994. *Excavated Bronze-Age Burial Mounds of North-east Yorkshire*. Northumberland Research Report 3.

Smith, R.A. 1924-5. The Perforated Axe-hammers of Britain. *Archaeologia* 75: 77–108.

Smith, R.A. 1931. *The Sturge Collection: an illustrated selection of flints from Britain bequeathed in 1919 by William Allen Sturge*. London: British Museum.

Smythe, J. 2006. An Early Bronze Age wristguard from Kent. *Kent Archaeological Society Newsletter* 69: 16.

Speed, G. 2010. *Excavations at Mitchell Laithes Farm, Ossett, West Yorkshire (Draft)*. Barnard Castle: NAA.

Spratt, D.A. 1982. The Cleave Dyke System. *Yorkshire Archaeological Journal* 54: 33–52.

Spratt, D.A. (ed.). 1993. *Prehistoric and Roman Archaeology of North-East Yorkshire.* CBA Research Report 87.

Stead, I.M. 1971. Beadlam Roman Villa: An Interim Report. *Yorkshire Archaeological Journal* 43: 178–86.

Sturrock, J. 1880. Notice of a jet necklace and urn of the food-vessel type found in a cist at Balcalk, Tealing and of the opening of Hatton cairn, Parish of Inverarity, Forfarshire. *Proceedings of the Society of Antiquaries of Scotland* 14 (1879–80): 260–7.

Switsur, R.V. and Jacobi, R.M. 1979. A radiocarbon chronology for the early postglacial stone industries of England and Wales. In Berger, R. and Suess, H.E. (eds), *Radiocarbon Dating,* 4168. London: University of California Press.

van der Vaart, S. 2009a. Beaker wrist-guards, how are they made and what was their use? Internal report, Land of Legends Lejre. Viewed 5 May 2021: <https://www.academia. edu/41075179/Beaker_wrist_guards_how_ are_ they_made_ and_what_was_ their_use_ Sasja_van_der_Vaart_assisted>.

van der Vaart, S. 2009b. Bell Beaker Wrist-guards Reconsidered. A research into their functionality and possible uses. Unpublished Bachelor dissertation. Faculty of Archaeology, Leiden University. Viewed 5 May 2021, <https://www.academia.edu/691452/Bell_Beaker_ wrist_guards_ reconsidered_ A_ research_ into_their_functionality_and_possible_uses>.

Vyner, B. 2001. The Earlier Prehistoric Pottery. In Roberts *et al.,* 149–52.

Vyner, B.E. 2008. Ceramic urns and small finds. In ASWYAS, Cross Farm, Stanbury: Archaeological Excavation, ASWYAS report, 1788.

Ward, T. 2021. *The Survey and Excavation of a Bronze Age and later landscape at Camps Reservoir, near Crawford, South Lanarkshire, 1992 and 1994.* Biggar: Biggar Archaeology Group. Viewed 2 September 2000, < http://biggararchaeology.org.uk/pdf/camps-reservoir-excavation-and-survey- report-1992-1004>.

Waughman, M. 2015. North East Yorkshire Mesolithic Project Phase 3 Final Report. Hartlepool: Tees Archaeology. Viewed 24 December 2020, <http://www.teesarchaeology.com/projects/ Mesolithic/ documents/FINALNYMesoPhase3report_Mar15.pdf>.

Waughman, M. 2017. Hunter-Gatherers in an Upland Landscape: The Mesolithic Period in North East Yorkshire. *Yorkshire Archaeological Journal* 89: 1–22.

Whitaker, T.D. 1816. A Catalogue and Description of the Natural and Artificial Rarities in this Musaeum. In Thoresby, R. 2nd edn. *Ducatus Leodiensis.* Leeds: Robinson, Son and Holdsworth.

Williams-Thorpe, O. and Thorpe, R.S. 1984. The distribution and sources of archaeological pitchstone in Britain. *Journal of Archaeological Science* 11(1): 1–34.

Wilson, P. 1995. The Yorkshire Moors in the Roman period: developments and directions. In Vyner, B. (ed.), *Moorland Monuments: Studies in the Archaeology of North-East Yorkshire in Honour of Raymond Hayes and Don Spratt,* 69–78. CBA Research Report 101.

Woodward, A. and Hunter, J. (eds). 2011. *An Examination of Prehistoric Stone Bracers from Britain.* Oxford: Oxbow.

Woodward, A. and Hunter, J., with Bukach, D., Needham, S.P. and Sheridan, J.A. 2015. *Ritual In Early Bronze Age Grave Goods: an examination of ritual and dress equipment from Chalcolithic and Early Bronze Age graves in England.* Oxford: Oxbow.

Wrigley, A. 1911. *Saddleworth: Its Prehistoric Remains.* Oldham: W.E. Clegg.

Wymer, J.J. (ed.). 1977. *Gazetteer of Mesolithic sites in England and Wales.* CBA Research Report 22.